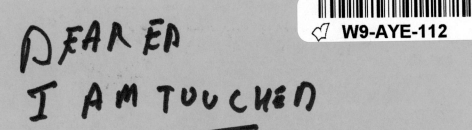

DEAR ED
I AM TOUCHED

THANK YOU WROTE
OUR CHAT IN MY

HONOR.
FRANK SINATRA

4/2/96

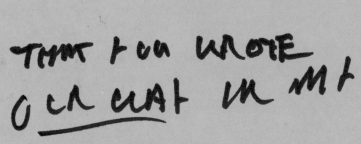

MR S
ENCLOSED
OF MY B4
I HAVE HIS LETTERS

OUR
WAY

IS FRANKS WAY

- TO A WONDERFUL
HUMAN BEING.
YOU WERE THE ONLY
ONE WHO STOOD BY
ME ALONG WITH
MR SINATRA

HIS DANCING WIFE
BARBARA   YOUR FRIEND
EDDY   RIGHT HERE
RAST EDDIE TO ETERNITY

ED SHIRAK, JR.

OUR
WAY

based on the song
"A Time That Was"

PUBLISHING

HOBOKEN • NEW JERSEY

1995

Words alone are not enough....Where strength and determination are clear, our words need merely to convey conviction, not belligerence. If we are strong, our strength will speak for itself. If we are weak, our words will be of no good.[1]

President John F. Kennedy
Undelivered speech:
Dallas, November 22, 1963

AUTHOR'S NOTE AND ACKNOWLEDGMENTS

I thank my parents for instilling in me the ethic of hard work that you don't get something for nothing. Mr. Mario Lepore has kept rolling truffles in spite of some terrible business decisions I have made along the way. Without his perspiration, I could never had the inspiration to write "Our Way." Thank you Jim Reardon and Bruce Stephen Foster, who wrote the beautiful words and music to "A Time That Was." To my Uncle James Galante who has made people happy through his cherished photos. To my grandparents, aunts and uncles who were all so very good to me.

I am grateful to the staff at the Hoboken Library where I spent much of my time researching the many books on Mr. Sinatra. My thanks to The Hudson Reporter and David Cogswell, for allowing me to use the article "Pursuing Sinatra From Here to Eternity." Also, without the wonderful people of Hoboken who took the time to recollect their memories of the Sinatras, I would not have been able to write this book. I am also very grateful to Eileen "Honey" O'Leary, who provided me with the beautiful picture on the front cover—her cherished possession given to her by Mr. Frank Sinatra. My special thanks to my chief editor, Mary Ann Villanella and Assistant Editor Debra Culhane. Finally, thank you Mr. Sinatra. Without your God given talent and the achievements in your lifetime, there would be no book.

It was a strange occurrence that "Our Way" was written based on the song, "A Time That Was," to honor Mr. Frank Sinatra. It wasn't planned to be; it just happened that way. The book includes: an overture, sonata, reprise, and encore with lyrics from the song to begin each chapter. I sought no major publishing firm to market this book since I wanted "Our Way" to come out of Hoboken just as Mr. Sinatra did—standing on his own merit and making it on his own. The writing, editing, typing, research and interviewing were all performed in Hoboken, as well as the financing for the project through Lepore's Chocolate. "Our Way" cannot speak for all the people in Hoboken because not even Frank Sinatra can be loved by everyone. However, when I began interviewing people from the city, they would all ask: "Did you read that book?" It was as if everyone in Hoboken referred to Kitty Kelley's unauthorized biography of Frank Sinatra, "His Way," as "that book." When I redirected their question and asked if they read "that book," the reply was overwhelmingly "No." The people I interviewed were incensed by "that book" as if it had disgraced the town. I spoke to over one hundred people and their reply would almost be identical: I never read "that book" nor would I ever buy "that book." I also never had any intention of reading "that book" until I had co-written the song "A Time That Was." When I felt Mr. Sinatra did not receive the tribute song that I delivered to him at The Sands on Nov. 18, I decided to write "Our Way." After reading the first 44 pages of "that book," I discovered beneath the facts lied the truth.

There would have been no book if I had personally reached Mr. Sinatra with his tribute presentation the night he performed at The Sands in Atlantic City. Although I was told he received the song by one of his staff members, I didn't believe it was true. Therefore, on November 22, 1994, I began to write.

Ed Shirak Jr.
April 16, 1995

To the greatest star in the world:
Mr. Francis Albert Sinatra
who inspired me to write this book.

Contents

Foreword

As I step to the conductor's podium and raise the baton, I would like to say before the overture begins that "Our Way" is based on "A Time That Was," Hoboken's tribute song to Mr. Frank Sinatra. On the cover of "Our Way," you see a brick arch which is the remains of 415 Monroe Street where Mr. Sinatra was born. The Arch of Frank was built by Mr. Pete Palmisano and Mr. Mark Septiembre to honor Mr. Sinatra, and "Our Way" was written to honor him in total truth.

Overture

No where else but Hoboken. Baseball and Sinatra. That's a lot of history for a mile square city! Baseball was born in this town and so was the greatest performer in the world, Mr Frank Sinatra. My credentials are much less impressive, yet nevertheless, I ran for Mayor of Hoboken in April of '93, but the outcome was not to my advantage. At fifty years of age, I have lived here all my life and consider myself one of the few remaining Hoboken buffalo.

During the campaign for Mayor, I attempted to create a hotel on the Hudson in Mr. Sinatra's honor, naming it "From here to Eternity." The idea came from an inspirational picture of Mr. Sinatra sitting on a pier in Hoboken staring out across the river and looking to New York as if he were dreaming what lay ahead of him in life. Under the picture, I also found a large poster of the old Yankee Stadium. Baseball and Sinatra immediately came to my mind. I envisioned a hotel that would include a theater for the performing arts along with a site for Hoboken's Baseball Hall of Fame. This splendid complex would create badly needed tax revenue for the city, which was twenty million dollars in debt as well as jobs for our people. Finally the long awaited tribute to the kid from Hoboken would become a reality.

On July 22, 1992, I miraculously came face to face with Mr. Francis Albert Sinatra at Medici Restaurant at the Sands Hotel in Atlantic City. When he spoke, I felt I had known him all my life, especially when he said; "I'm from Hoboken." However, when my efforts failed to deliver a hotel on the Hudson, I conceived a tribute song in Mr. Sinatra's honor. I entitled it, "A Time That Was." It tells the story of his life while living in Hoboken and his rise to stardom as the greatest entertainer in the world. The manner in which my business partner Mario Lepore and I delivered his against all odds presentation is a bizarre story that I think you will find very interesting. Because I was never confident that he received the tribute song, I decided to write this story.

After reading the first forty-four pages of Kitty Kelley's book, "His Way," the unauthorized biography of Mr. Sinatra, the real purpose finally became clear. "Our Way" was written in Mr. Sinatra's honor to simply tell the truth. It is about prophets and profits as well as ordinary and extra ordinary people. And finally, it is our way to tell Mr. Sinatra how proud we are of the contributions he has made to the world through his wonderful music, and how his city loves such a caring and giving human being.

Abraham Lincoln once said: "Always bear in mind, your own resolution to succeed is more important than any one thing." Therefore, I hope I have succeeded in explaining why I felt so compelled to write this book.

UNCLE JIMMY
(from the Galante collection)

*"While our soldiers marched away
and boarded ships that sail to war"*

Uncle Jimmy Galante celebrating his
61st birthday, July 17, 1963. He's the
guy responsible for this story since Mr.
Sinatra was his hero. You can see a
similar arch in back of Uncle Jimmy
resembling "The Arch of Frank" on the
front cover of "Our Way."

THE VISION *(from the Galante collection)*

*"The Hudson River flows along the town
where he was born"*

A young teenage Sinatra gazes out from a pier in Hoboken
wondering where life's destiny leads him. This picture
inspired the tribute of: Sinatra's "From Here to Eternity."

OLD YANKEE STADIUM *(from the Galante collection)*

"Daddy's and rainbows baseball and heroes never die"
From the song: "Baseball Was Born In This Town" by Jim Reardon

Under the picture of Mr. Sinatra looking across the river to New York, I discovered a poster of Old Yankee
Stadium with a signature of Joe DiMaggio to Jimmy Galante. Baseball and Sinatra instantly came to my
mind since baseball was born in this town.

OUR WAY

based on the song
"A Time That Was"

Sonata

The Hudson River flows along the town where he was born. He walked the streets in a young boys dream trying to make it on his own, where we still hear those children Christmas morn and the flags in parades and blowing horns. The champagne overflowed New Years Eve in every bar, while our soldiers marched away and boarded ships that sail to war.

This is a true story of "A Time That Was" and a time that still is! I write this book in the honor of Mr. Francis Albert Sinatra, who was born in Hoboken December 12, 1915 and baptized on April 12, 1916 at St. Francis Holy Roman Catholic Church. His father, Anthony Sinatra, Godmother, Ana Gatto, and Godfather, Frank Garrick, were present, while his mother Natalie lay ill at home recovering from bearing a son that nearly cost her life. No where else but in Hoboken could this book have been written.

In March of '92, I discovered many rare Sinatra negatives in my parents basement, which belonged to my Uncle James Vincent Galante, a World War II army hero and a deceased lithographer by trade. Inspired by a picture of a young teenage Sinatra overlooking the Hudson River from Hoboken, I began my quest. My initial vision was to pay ultimate tribute to the world's greatest performer by creating a hotel on the Hudson and naming it "Sinatra's From Here To Eternity." It would be a magnificent hotel, which would include a Sinatra theater for the performing arts along with a special site for Hoboken's Baseball Hall of Fame, since baseball was born in this town. My three year attempt to get to Mr. Sinatra met with overwhelming setbacks and rejection taking me to the point of financial insolvency and ultimately police arrest. During this time, I had already announced my candidacy for Mayor of the City of Hoboken so I could not turn back in spite of having no money to wage a formidable campaign. The lawyers whom I had retained to represent me led to my conviction and depleted the ten thousand dollars I personally managed to save to run for Mayor of the mile square city.

When I called Sid Marks, the famous radio broadcaster, who airs all the great Sinatra music throughout the country to tell him of my idea, he politely and professionally told me: "No one gets to Sinatra not even me anymore. The President can't even get to Sinatra." His statement made my own resolution to succeed only greater and four months later I and my business partner, Mario Lepore, came face to face with the world's greatest performer at I' Medici Restaurant at the Sands Hotel in Atlantic City. The encounter with Mr. Sinatra was real and close up yet mystical in his conversation, and I will never forget it as long as I live! I will explain later how the three kids from Hoboken met. As for now, I can only say that "Our Way" is about courage, prophets, and profits as well as ordinary and extraordinary people. It is about miracles and total truth. It tells about Hoboken's tribute song to Mr. Frank Sinatra, entitled "A Time That Was," which was written by Jim Reardon, Bruce Stephen Foster, and the author of this book. Our objective was to make Mr. Sinatra happy by a tribute in song. At this moment as I write, I am still not certain if he genuinely received our gift, which was commissioned by Mayor Anthony Russo on November 3, 1994.

I began my journey using the inspirational words from St. Peter, "Quo Vadis Domini?" or, "Which Way Lord?" Pope John Paul II dedicated his papacy on the strength of St. Peter's words when he was ordained Pontiff more than seventeen years ago. In his most recent book, "Crossing the Threshold of Hope," His Holiness encourages us to "Be Not Afraid," the very words Jesus spoke to his disciples? With those profound statements in mind, I found inner strength, but my mission was unclear at times as to what I could do for Mr. Sinatra and our city. I wanted Hoboken to be a model to all the cities throughout the country how we as a people can benefit if we work together in harmony for a common cause. You may at this time be asking yourself: Who is this guy to write a book in Mr. Sinatra's honor and who is he to speak for Hoboken? I can only respond by saying that since I ran for Mayor in April of '93, I feel I have found the manner to serve the people by telling Mr. Sinatra in "Our Way" how the City has always felt about him. We simply love him! I will try as best I can to get this message across for our City and earnestly hope I represent it nobly in my efforts.

Earlier I had indicated that at times my path to Sinatra was unclear and uncertain. Therefore, when I returned home on Saturday from the Sands Hotel in Atlantic City, I did not feel certain that Mr. Sinatra received Hoboken's tribute in song. I will elaborate on this major point later in my story, on happenings that might have occurred Friday evening while Sinatra slept. Suddenly, I began to realize that the only way I would really know if Mr. Sinatra received our gift was to write this book. The path was finally clear with a definitiveness of purpose.

When I began my research in the Hoboken Library, I began reading the infamous book written by Kitty Kelley, "His Way." Mr. Sinatra fought relentlessly to keep the book from being printed because Sinatra Enterprises felt the writings contained numerous untruths. As I read the first forty-four pages which was exclusively devoted to his life in Hoboken, I saw why he protested so vehemently. Kitty Kelley is a talented writer and presented credible facts but with-held significant qualitative information. In other words, the book smacked of prolific sophistry. I will support this statement later in the only way—our way. After page forty-four, I had to go no further because if sophism reigns supreme at the on start of a book, how can the remainder of a story carry any credible significance?

If you go beyond the facts, you immediately realize that Natalie Sinatra was a prophet. She had vision and was a woman ahead of her times as well as ahead of most men and one of the most influential people in the City of Hoboken. Dolly was a woman who fought for the rights of men and women. She helped the poor, loved people, and people loved Dolly Sinatra. "Our Way" will be living testimony from people in Hoboken who remember her as well as the Sinatras. They will come forward and speak the truth about a woman of courage, and I will tell the story on how my purpose shifted from an attempt to honor Mr. Sinatra with a hotel on the Hudson, to a tribute song, to ultimately discovering my real mission—speaking the truth. This is our way to tell the entire story, and it is my way of thanking God for showing me the way to "Be Not Afraid."

The great First Lady, Eleanor Roosevelt once said, "You gain courage, strength and confidence by every experience when you really stop and look fear in the face." Dolly Sinatra had courage and looked fear in the face every day of her life. Mr. Sinatra continues to perform with courageous inner strength singing to the world and making people happy. The Sonata is through.

And now, may I tell you the story, our way for you?

While our soldiers marched away
and boarded ships that sail to war

CHAPTER 1

My Uncle was a War Hero

In 1917 the United States entered World War I, and no American port played a greater wartime role than Hoboken. More than one million American troops had sailed from Hoboken and an equal number landed here after the war. Heaven, Hell or Hoboken by Christmas was the battle cry! Although the city did not become a major port of embarkation as it had been in the first great conflict, its piers played a significant part in wartime shipping in World War II.[4]

My uncle was a war hero in World War II and became a successful businessman beginning as a lithographer. He embarked from our piers in 1942 and witnessed savage fighting in Anzio. James Vincent Galante was wounded in action and saw many of his friends die in Italy. He received the Silver Star, Bronze Star, and Purple Heart for meritorious acts on the battle fields. After being hospitalized in Italy, he was shipped to the Phillipines, since the war with Japan still raged in full fury. He did not see action in the South Pacific since the war ended when Hiroshima and Nagasaki were decimated by Harry S. Truman's decision to drop the atomic bomb. After the war, my uncle served as a foster father to my cousins, Charles and Carol Romano, when my Uncle Charles Romano died suddenly of a heart attack at forty years of age. My Aunt Helen (Shirak) Romano will tell later in the story how my uncle and Dolly Sinatra sang and danced at his father's house on Clinton Street. These were happy times with good people and strong family values.

Uncle Jimmy loved life and was very patriotic. The war, however, left emotional scars that never left him. When my brother Ken and I or one of my cousins would ask him to tell us stories about the war, he would change the subject immediately. I now serve as my Aunt Florence's legal guardian ever since my uncle passed away more than ten years ago. I remember receiving the call from Englewood Hospital that my uncle was in a car accident. He told the nurse to call Butch, which is my nickname, to come pick him up. My uncle had gone to a Lion's Club party and unfortunately had too much to drink. On the way home he lost control of his vehicle and hit a telephone pole and was taken for treatment. As soon as I arrived, he walked out from the emergency room with an intern accompanying him. Shaken and still covered with blood from the accident, his first words were: "Butch, don't tell Aunt Florry." I allayed his fear by assuring him that I would not.

Instantly, he had a flashback of World War II and the battle field at Anzio, Italy. His eyes twitched and his body trembled and he began to tell his horror story. As if he were back in a foxhole experiencing enemy shelling, he began reliving a night that haunted him throughout the remainder of his life.

"We're really going to get it tonight Joe. Yeah, I feel it Joe. It's really going to be bad tonight." As he spoke, he began ducking, bobbing and weaving as if the impact of the shells were causing his entire body to shake from exploding bombs around him. He then let out a horrifying scream: "Oh God, Oh God! it's the kid, it's the kid! His whole neck is hanging out. His neck is all blown out!" He then began crying. During his flashback of the battle scene, I felt helpless and hoped the doctor knew how to console my uncle.

However, in an instant, Private Galante vicariously left Anzio, Italy and once again became Uncle Jimmy. The doctor told me not to worry, stating in a casual manner, "He's an old war vet, shell shocked you know." I then asked, "are you all right Uncle Jimmy?" He assured me he was, but once again pleaded with me not to tell Aunt Florry. I brought him home, and the incident had passed. I now know that my aunt had lived with my uncle's internal nightmare for as long as they were married, but she never said a word.

On September 10, 1984 I received a call from a Riverview Hospital in Red Bank, New Jersey. This time I was requested to identify my uncle's body. He was buried in Calvary Veteran's Cemetery having the military funeral he deserved. During his life my uncle loved Frank Sinatra and collected many rare photos of him. Since he was a lithographer by trade, he spent a large portion of his time reproducing every negative or picture he could obtain of his singing idle. His hobby gave him extreme pleasure showing people rare photographs of Mr. Sinatra. Little did I know that my uncle's cherished collection would begin my journey and lead me into combat for another cause.

As a young boy before the war, my uncle was a delivery boy at Balboa's pizza parlor in Hoboken. Dolly Sinatra and her husband Marty, along with young Frank Sinatra, would frequent Balboa's to enjoy pizza and listen to Frank's music on the juke box. Joe 'Gigi' Lisa, who was a waiter at Balboa's at the time, will tell you his recollections of Dolly and Frank later in the book. My uncle never met the Sinatras, but it is good to know that the Sinatras now know about Uncle Jimmy. Until this day I carry his photo handbag with pictures and memories of him and Frank Sinatra.

In my right hand I carry an attache case given to me by my Aunt Marie Sirocka. My Uncle Frank Sirocka attended school with Frank Sinatra and both graduated from David E. Rue Junior High School. You can see, in an original photograph in the book, how Frank Sinatra stood right behind my uncle on graduation day. My Aunt Marie (Pflug) Sirocka tells me that Frank and Frank were in constant trouble throwing books on the floor in Mrs. Ginsberg's class. How close can you get to Frank Sinatra unless your name is Frank Sirocka?

On a more somber note, my Aunt Florence Galante suffered a nervous breakdown six months after my uncle passed away. She was committed to Marlboro State Psychiatric Hospital when she began hallucinating about the war in Japan. We were never informed that she was taken to Marlboro until the next day. The judge committed her when the police were not able to reach us because they were dialing a wrong number that my aunt had recorded in her telephone book. When you are committed to a state institution, it is extremely difficult to get out, unless you have somebody working daily in your behalf. After visiting my aunt for seven days in Marlboro, I obtained her release. I then assumed legal guardianship over her with the consent of my father, Aunt Helen (Shirak) Romano and my Uncle Richard, who are my aunt's surviving blood relatives.

In March of 1990 my aunt had a second nervous breakdown. Because she was hallucinating and living by herself, I sought professional help. I committed her to the Carrier Foundation that specializes in treating schizophrenia. After one month of treatment, she was released and returned home. The Doctor at the hospital made it clear that she would have to be medicated for the rest of her life. I was also told that she might develop Parkinson's Disease from the use of the medication Haldol, which is an anti-hallucinatory drug. Once a month I would take her for outpatient treatment, and while she stopped hallucinating, her personality began to change. She lost her vitality and walked in a stupefied manner and in a short time developed Parkinson's Disease. When she spoke, her face would become contorted, and her mouth would move to the side of her face. She also began losing her muscular skeletal coordination. I spoke with Doctor Dengrove and asked him what would the consequences be if I decided to stop administering the medication. He told me that all the hallucinatory symptoms would reappear with "incipience."

Since I would rather see her hallucinate than to experience the pitiful life she was now living, I went against the prognostication of the doctor. I stopped administering the drug Haldol, and miraculously Aunt Florence returned to a normal state.

When I called Dr. Dengrove to inform him, he had no explanation other than: "Sometimes these things happen." Because I had faith in my aunt to recover by her own will, she responded! Almost four years later, she is doing extremely well without any form of medication which I consider a small miracle.

CHAPTER 2

Baseball and Sinatra

No where else but Hoboken. Baseball and Sinatra! That's America to me. On June 19, 1846, the first organized game of baseball was played at Elysian Fields located at eleventh and Hudson Streets.[4] On May 3, 1990, I received a personal letter from Mayor Patrick Pasculli inviting me to partake in Hoboken's first annual Baseball Day Celebration. Finally, Hoboken would be celebrating this memorable event. This was also the year our Babe Ruth Team won the city and division championship. It took us nine years, but our kids finally did it! As coach of Lepores, I was extremely proud of a team who won against all odds.

Since I had been one of the founders of the organized Babe Ruth League, I wanted to do more than just participate in Baseball Day and decided Hoboken should have a Baseball tribute song. At the time I was the business manager of a singer and songwriter named Jimmy Reardon. In 1989 Jim had written a tribute song entitled "Harry" in honor of Harry Chapin, who during his life, gave half of his earnings to charity to fight against world hunger. Because of Jim's achievement, he was invited to Carnegie Hall the evening the late Harry Chapin was to be honored.

When I called Jimmy, I explained my idea and gave him a brief history about baseball. I told him that baseball was born in this town. He stopped me from going further and replied: "Ed, that's the title. That's it! "Baseball Was Born in This Town." Jim came to Hoboken and wrote the song on June 1, 1990 and recorded it at Emaeus Studio in Point Pleasant, New Jersey on June 7 th.

As President of the Hoboken Babe Ruth League, I thought the tribute song would be welcomed by the Mayor and the political authorities who were organizing the baseball day activities. I did not expect to encounter arrogance and resistance from a lawyer named Steven Speiser, who was the head of the American Heritage Baseball Association. He and Mayor Pasculli were jointly in charge of the newly created organization. In our initial meeting, he described me as a man with "no letter head" and knew immediately that he didn't think much of a Babe Ruth baseball coach and an owner of a chocolate shop. Since the production of the song cost in excess of two thousand dollars and was our gift to the city, I was not too happy in the manner in which he viewed me.

Before founding Lepore's Chocolate, I had been an Executive Search Consultant with over twelve years experience in Human Resource Management with my own firm Philip Edward Associates Inc. This is not to impress you but to impress upon you how some people will form a judgement on the basis of a seal or legal certificate. "You don't have letterhead, Ed." This was Mr. Speiser's remark when I first met with him to ask him to listen to the baseball song, which was soon to become Hoboken's Baseball Anthem. To a lawyer letterhead is the legal clout they possess in a seal to get things accomplished that, in their view, the ordinary person can not achieve.

When he reluctantly invited me to sit down, I told him about the song. He told me to leave a copy of the tape and that he would listen to it when he had the chance. Enraged over his smug demeanor, I rose from my seat storming from the office refusing to leave the song. I then stopped my exit and forcefully replied: "Look Steve,

listen to the song now or forget about it!" I placed my cassette
player on his desk and pushed the play button. Steve began to
listen to "Baseball Was Born in This Town." When he heard the
chorus line "Cooperstown may claim the Hall of Fame but this is
where the first game was played," he began to smile. Suddenly, he
stopped everything he was preoccupied with because he knew he
had something of quality for Hoboken's first Baseball Day.
Jimmy Reardon became a valuable person in Mr. Speiser's eyes,
and he requested to thank him personally for the song. At this
time no one knew that Jim Reardon would be singing for Tony
Bennett, who is Mr. Sinatra's favorite singer, at the posh supper
club, On the Waterfront in Hoboken only three months later. In
1952, scenes from the academy award winning movie, "On The
Waterfront" were filmed at the bar starring Marlon Brando and
Eva Marie Saint.

    June 19, 1990 proved to be a very special day for Hoboken
and the song, "Baseball Was Born in This Town." We were to be
included in the program, and the baseball song was to be one of the
highlights of the day. Steven Speiser told us that he would have the
Mayor commission the song. Translated politically, it meant City
Hall created the idea to have a baseball tribute song. Because we
desperately wanted the song included in the Baseball Day
ceremonies, I allowed the politicians to take the credit. We decided
to print up T shirts which read: 'No where else but Hoboken' on
the front, and 'Baseball and Sinatra' on the back. The people who
bought the shirts were proud displaying baseball and Mr. Sinatra's
name while celebrating Baseball Day in the small historic city.

    Many dignitaries were on hand including: John Honey
Romano, the All Star catcher of the Cleveland Indians, who was
born in Hoboken, as well as Bobby Thomson, the man who hit the
shot heard round the world when the Giants beat the Dodgers at
the Polo Grounds for the National League Pennant in 1950.
Governor James Florio also attended and officially declared
Hoboken the true birthplace of Baseball by a State Proclamation.
Bands from New York and New Jersey marched down Washington

Street, which is the main thoroughfare of the city. All of Hoboken's children who played in the Minor League, Little League and Babe Ruth League, along with the varsity baseball team marched proudly through our historic town. Finally, Jimmy Reardon sang "Baseball Was Born in This Town" to a capacity stadium in Fourth Street Park, home of the Hoboken Little League, and the rest was history. In Hoboken's Baseball Anthem, Jim pays special tribute to Mr. Sinatra. Can you find the line in the song?

"BASEBALL WAS BORN IN THIS TOWN"

Well it all started here more than a century ago
When Elysian Grass was young just beginning to grow
They played fair and square with family and friends in
*   the sun,*
It was only a game at the time. It didn't matter who won.
With a ball and a glove or some wood in your hands,
*   you could*
feel like a legend, more than a man.

Chorus

Baseball was born in this town
Here in the heart of Hoboken
Cooperstown may claim the Hall of Fame
But this is where the first game was played.
And I'm proud to say-hey, hey baseball was born in this town.
I heard someone say, it was a very good year.
When hearts were still young and there was nothing to fear
Long before the Civil War life was so much simpler in
*   those days.*
You could buy some soda and popcorn with the nickel that
*   you saved*
The American dream on the field of green lives on forever,
*   whatever the cost.*

Repeat Chorus

To this very day a child sits next to his father
With a ball and a glove and a twinkle in his eyes
And he truly believes in his God, home and country,
Daddy's and rainbows, baseball and heroes never die.

Baseball was born in this town.
Here in the heart of Hoboken.
Cooperstown may claim the Hall of Fame
But this is where the first game was played.
And I'm proud to say-hey, hey, baseball was born,
    baseball was born
baseball was born in this town. Yes it was!

Up until Jim began to sing, I never knew if he was going to get the chance to perform on that sultry summer day. The munisicrats would give us a time when Jim would sing after the political speeches and pomp and circumstance were through. As fate would have it, Governor Florio's body guard was standing next to me with Jim on the playing field while the Governor's helicopter was hovering above as he prepared to land outside of the ballfield. The guard called out to me and said: "Hey are you with the singer?" I replied, "Yes." He instructed me to have Jim begin singing as soon as the Governor entered the stadium. Instead of the predictable introductory speech by a local official, the unpredictable happened. Mr. Reardon began to sing. The stadium came alive with people singing and rhythmic hand clapping, and the Governor was warmly received. When the ceremonies were completed, Bob Bodsner, senior producer of Phoenix Cable TV who does all baseball broadcasts throughout the country, began taping us live and proceeded to ask us if he could use the song for TV networks. It was a very proud moment for Jim Reardon. During this time, Jim presented Governor Florio with a copy of the Baseball song. The Governor's eyes glowed in what I perceived

GRADUATION DAY 1931 AT DAVID E. RUE JR. H.S.

(Courtesy of Marie (Pflug) Sirocca)

"Will the child you once were,
come along with me now and take
the last carousel ride"

From the song: "Last Painted Pony"
by Bruce Stephen Foster

On the steps at A.J. Demarest H.S. is Mr. Frank Sinatra with my uncle Frank Sirocka standing next to each other. You can't get any closer to Frank Sinatra unless your name is Frank Sirocka. Frank and Frank stand in the middle of the boys in a zoom-in picture. Who is Frank Sinatra and Frank Sirocka: Hint, they are dressed very much alike.

NOWHERE ELSE BUT HOBOKEN, BASEBALL AND SINATRA
(Photo by Al Palmieri)

"Cooperstown may claim the Hall of Fame, but this is where the first game was played."

FIRST ANNUAL BASEBALL DAY IN HOBOKEN JUNE 19, 1990
(photo by Al Palmieri)

"Once the Governor himself took a picture with me"
From the song: "Last Painted Pony"

Jim Reardon proudly presents Governor James Florio with a copy of the song "Baseball Was Born In This Town," without having letterhead.

THE SHOT HEARD 'ROUND THE WORLD *(Photo by Al Palmieri)*
"I heard someone say it was a very good year"

When Bobby Thomson homered for the New York Giants to beat the Brooklyn Dodgers for the National League Pennant in 1950, the memorable event became known as "The Shot Heard 'Round The World." Bobby Thomson, N.Y. Giant great, pens a rare signature on Hoboken's official logo for Jim Reardon for writing "Baseball Was Born In This Town."

to be genuine gratitude. At the same time, cameramen were taping us as we were being interviewed by TV broadcasters about the song. We couldn't believe what was happening. Jim Reardon was once again requested to sing the baseball song and the celebration lasted from 12:00 in the afternoon until 12:00 in the evening.

I had rented a limousine that evening just in case we got lucky, meaning that just once the hard work to produce a song would pay off. As Jim Reardon, Mario Lepore and I left the stadium in our 15 year old rented limo, people lined up with their children trying to shake Jimmy's hand for what he had done in song for our City. As we began to pull away, a young boy raced behind the limo shouting "Jimmy, Jimmy." Jim tried to have the limo driver stop because he knew the boy wanted his autograph. Unfortunately, the driver accelerated and we left the ballfield arriving at Trapani's Restaurant, where Jim promised to perform that evening.

Two weeks later, Jim performed at the Nite Spot, which was named the old Town Lunch, when Mr. Sinatra lived in Hoboken. Jim sang to a capacity audience, finaleing with "Baseball was Born in This Town." Because of Jim's tribute song, a bronze plaque was placed outside of Lepore's Chocolate donated by the people of Hoboken and it reads:

> *On June 7, 1990, Jimmy Reardon wrote "Baseball was Born in This Town." Cooperstown may claim the Hall of Fame but this is where the first game was played.*

Four days later, a letter arrived at City Hall from Governor James Florio. The letter, however, was directed to Lepore's Chocolate with special attention: to Mr. Jim Reardon. At 11:00 am, a messenger brought the letter to our store. When I saw the letterhead from the Governor of the State of New Jersey, I remembered Steve Speiser's comment to me, "You have no letterhead, Ed." I opened the letter and it read:

Dear Jim:
Just a note to say thanks for the song and for your help
in making my day in Hoboken such a great one. Please give
my best to all our friends.

                                        Sincerely,
                                        Governor Jim Florio

I guess the Governor liked the song or should I say Hoboken's Baseball Anthem. Two weeks later, Mel Allen, the immortal voice of the New York Yankees told the story of Baseball Day on "This Day in Baseball," on the Mets pre game show that aired throughout the country. The song was given special air time by Mr. Bob Bodsner, the gentlemen who produced Hoboken's first Baseball Day for Channel 9. Because he knew we made a genuine contribution without requesting money, he made certain those who viewed "This Day in Baseball" knew the true story about where the seeds of organized baseball were planted.

The irony of the bronze plaque that was dedicated to Mr. Reardon for writing the baseball song lies just one block away. By one block away I mean, Hoboken is a mile square. We call the streets blocks, and there are sixteen blocks in which forty two thousand residents live. One block away is a bronze plaque dedicated to the famous Stephen Foster, who lived and wrote many of his notable songs while living in Hoboken. Some of his wonderful songs were: "Old Kentucky Home," "Jeannie with the Light Brown Hair," and "Way Down Upon the Swanee River." Bruce Stephen Foster, the great, grandnephew of the famous Stephen Foster would co-write with Jim Reardon "A Time That Was," Hoboken's tribute to Frank Sinatra two years later.

Just six months after Baseball Day, Jim became emotionally ill. He began to suffer from depression because of severe financial problems and was committed to Ancora Psychiatric Hospital for attempting suicide on two occasions. As Jim's condition deteriorated, there seemed to be little hope that he would ever return to a normal state of mind. We were three days away from

Hoboken's Second Annual Baseball Day celebration when I decided to visit Jim for the final time. When I spoke to him, he just looked and stared with no expression. I asked, "How are you, Jimmy?" He then stated, "I just want to die, Ed." We both sat in the patient's visiting room for about 15 minutes in complete silence. I then took a deep breath and said to myself, "Please God let this work." I then told him that it would be Baseball Day in three days. I made him recall what a very special day it was as we rode our 15 year old limo through the town after he had met the Governor, and how wonderful the people felt because of his song just one year ago. I told him it was with deep regret that I would have to get another singer to sing the baseball anthem.

When I said another singer, I began to see traces of the old Jimmy Reardon. His blue eyes flashed with life, and I detected a tinge of performer's jealousy. He stood up erectly and told me he would go before a board of five nurses and doctor's and explain to them that he just wanted one day leave from the hospital to sing the baseball song in Hoboken. He told me to call him the next day, and he would let me know if he would be allowed to perform. At this time I didn't know if I had hurt him deeper emotionally since I didn't believe he would be singing at Baseball Day even though I prayed for a miracle. When I called Jim the next day, he had miraculously convinced the medical staff and was escorted to Hoboken by a few close friends who promised to bring him back after he had sung in Hoboken.

When Jim arrived at the ballfield on Baseball Day, he looked like a different person. He had lost fifty pounds and had not sung in almost six months. When he strapped on his guitar, he seemed unsure of himself and appeared visibly shaken. It was encouraging yet difficult to see such a talented entertainer fighting desperately to regain the command of the stage he once had. I recalled just six months ago how he had entertained the great Tony Bennett at "On the Waterfront" Restaurant in Hoboken. As Mr. Bennett left the restaurant that evening, he personally shook Jimmy's hand telling him how much he had enjoyed his singing. Now, on

Baseball Day, we waited anxiously to see if Jim would sing again. When he began, there was a raspy quiver in his voice. But as people began their rhythmic clapping to the baseball song, Jim's voice grew strong. After he completed Hoboken's Baseball Anthem, he was met with a crescendo of applause. After his success, he was taken to lunch with some old friends and then driven back to the hospital.

Life became worth living for Jim Reardon once again, and he was released from Ancora Psychiatric Hospital shortly after Baseball Day. He would complete the first version of "A Time That Was" on December 12, 1992, on Mr. Sinatra's seventy seventh birthday. Jim is now singing better than ever and hopes to perform in Las Vegas as Roy Orbeson in the famous production, "Legends." I hope someday Jim Reardon, Bruce Stephen Foster and I will be together again to honor the greatest performer in the world, Mr. Frank Sinatra. No where else but Hoboken. Baseball and Sinatra. That's America to me!

Let him tell you his story,
Let him sing once again for you

CHAPTER 3

Mario, Frank and Me
at I'Medici

In January of 92, I began to consider running for Mayor of the City of Hoboken. I believed very deeply that the city could serve as a model for all the cities throughout the country by demonstrating how we could market the history and culture of the people. I always felt that Baseball and Sinatra could be sold with class and tradition that would benefit the city, the people and Mr. Frank Sinatra. During this time I had no idea on how to achieve bringing Mr. Sinatra and Hoboken back together, especially when Kitty Kelley's book, "His Way," appeared in the bookstores nationally in 1986. When I told my father of my intentions to run for Mayor, he reminded me of my Uncle Jimmy's cherished photo collection of Frank Sinatra, which had been placed in "an old trunk" in my parent's basement when my uncle passed away in 1984.

As I walked down the stairs anticipating a nostalgic experience, I had no idea what treasures I would find when I opened "that old trunk." When I lifted the lid, I was astonished to see how comprehensive my uncle's photo collection was of Mr.

Sinatra. The first photo I discovered was Mr. Sinatra as a young
man staring mystically across the Hudson River as if he was
dreaming of what lay ahead for him in life. Young Frank was on a
pier sitting at Old Elysian Field where the first organized game of
baseball was played on June 19, 1846. Ten years later, the Maxwell
House Coffee Plant would be built upon Elysian Fields where
young Frank once sat. Under the photo of Mr. Sinatra was a large
poster of the Old Yankee Stadium with a signed autograph to my
Uncle Jimmy from Joe DiMaggio. I was so excited by my newly
found treasure that I dashed across the street to show our neighbor
Mrs. Barbara Yeger. As she was knitting like Madame De Farge
from Charles Dicken's "A Tale of Two Cities," Mrs. Yeger glanced
up at me and stated unemotionally, "Let's hope those pictures are
not a curse, Eddie." I had no idea that Barbara's portentous remark
had set the stage for what lay ahead in reaching Mr. Frank Sinatra.
When I told my Aunt Florence Galante about the photos, she
instructed me to give the contents to the Sinatra family. She told
me, "They don't belong to me; they belong to the Sinatras. Please
see that Mr. Sinatra gets them." Being her legal guardian from her
emotional illness, I knew what my mission was. I told her I would
get to Sinatra on her behalf, which seemed an impossible task to
me at the time.

   While jogging along Sinatra Drive in Hoboken the very next
day, I looked up at the Old Maxwell House building. The company
had just relocated their facilities to Jacksonville Florida, which
marked an end of an era for industrial manufacturing in Hoboken.
In the forties and fifties, Hoboken flourished with many industries
which meant jobs for its people. Now Hoboken had finally met the
fate of all the cities—no jobs, high taxes, and municipal bankruptcy.
As I jogged closer to the old plant on the Hudson, Sinatra's "From
Here to Eternity" flashed into my mind. The old Maxwell House
sign that shined across the Hudson River to New York would now
light up the waterfront with Sinatra's "From Here to Eternity."
The old photo of young Frank mystically gazing out across the
Hudson had given me the idea since it was the very site where

FROM HERE TO ETERNITY DOESN'T SEEM SO FAR WHEN WE FEEL SO CLOSE TO YOU

In 1954 Mr. Sinatra received the Academy Award for the best supporting actor portraying Maggio in the movie, "From Here to Eternity." This great movie won eight Academy Awards which included: best directing, editing, sound, cinematography, writing, best supporting actress, best supporting actor, as well as the 1953 movie of the year. Mr. Sinatra's performance as Private Angelo Maggio is still considered one of the hallmark performances in acting. He auditioned for the role and was selected by the head of Columbia Pictures, Harry Cohn, to portray Maggio. From then to present, he has enjoyed a career of unparalleled success.

On page 21 of "Our Way", the book states, by my own editing mistake, that Mr. Sinatra portrayed Maggio in 1950. Although this is chronologically incorrect, it is a fact that Mr. Sinatra was obsessed with playing the character Maggio after he read James Jones's novel, "From Here to Eternity" two years before the movie was made. When the book was written in 1951, it was as if he were destined to play the role in which he fit so well.

If fate dictates a second printing, the appropriate date change will be made.

Ed Shirak Jr.

Ed Shirak Jr.

June 7, 1995

Maxwell House was built ten years later, while Mr. Sinatra went on to win an academy award portraying Maggio in 1950 in the classic movie "From Here to Eternity." I saw it clearly. Now the world would be coming to Hoboken in Mr. Sinatra's honor, and Maggio would live on forever. Yes, a hotel on the Hudson. It would be magnificent, which would include a Sinatra theater for the performing arts along with a special site for Baseball's Hall of Fame since baseball was born in this town. This would mean renewed tax revenue for the city, as well as jobs for our people. Baseball, Sinatra, and Hoboken would finally be coming together for recognition, tribute and pride. All roads would definitely lead to Hoboken.

When the idea took hold in my mind, I called a close business confidant who had personal contact with corporate executives at General Foods, which owned Maxwell House. I arranged a meeting with them, told them of my idea, and showed them the Sinatra photos. I met with Mr. Frank Czwerski, Manager of Real Estate Operations and received a ballpark figure for the entire Maxwell House facility. I was shocked to find out that Philip Morris, which owned General Foods and Maxwell House, only wanted Four million dollars for the entire complex. This is almost one third of the Hoboken Waterfront! I arranged meetings with corporate backers selling them on the idea of a hotel in Hoboken. I had the opportunity to meet Governor Florio in Hoboken when he was campaigning for re-election in 1992 and gave him the proposal. The Governor had remembered Lepore's from Baseball Day, when we had produced the song, "Baseball Was Born in This Town", which made my meeting with him a lot easier. I was directed to the Economic Development Agency for possible monetary backing on the project. I had done the basic research for this major under-taking. The next step and the most difficult was how do I meet Sinatra. Mr. Frank Totaro, who bartends at Michael's Restaurant in Hoboken, suggested I call the famous radio broadcaster, Sid Marks in Philadelphia, who has been playing Sinatra music for many years. Sid, at first, was tough to reach. But through determination and perseverance, I finally spoke with him over the phone. He told me "no one gets to Sinatra these days, not even the President." He was polite and professional while we spoke at length about my idea. He wished me success but again stressed that "nobody gets to Sinatra."

The following week the Onieals 5 Mile Run was taking place in Hoboken. By what I feel was a small miracle, the head TV cameraman for Tina Sinatra's production, "Sinatra" stumbled into Lepore's Chocolate looking for Onieals Tavern to register for the five mile run and saw a picture of Sinatra displayed over our cash register. He replied, "I see you like Sinatra." I thought nothing of his comment at the time and simply said, "Yeah, we think he is great." He then saw the photo of Sinatra sitting on the banks of the Hudson staring out at New York. With great interest he commented, "this is an amazing photo. How would you like to meet Tina Sinatra? She is right down the street filming."

In an instant, we were off to meet Tina and present her with a picture of Mr. Sinatra that she had never seen. She shouted to her aid very excitedly, "Doesn't daddy look just like Philip?" Tina was referring to Philip Casanoff, the young actor she chose to play the lead role as Mr. Sinatra in her five hour mini-series called, "Sinatra." She told me the next day she would come to Lepore's and pick up the pictures and negatives that I had acquired from the Galante Estate. Since I wanted to make certain that Tina would come to the store, Mr. Lepore and I decided that he would run with Stan Feldman, Tina's cameraman, and I would stay at the store to meet Tina. The next day Tina wandered the streets of Hoboken looking for Lepore's on a futile mission—lost in Hoboken. By 6:30 Saturday evening, I sensed Tina wasn't coming. I had no idea on how to get in touch with her but took a lucky guess. I was planning to see Sinatra in concert at the Sands on July 23rd and knew that Ramada owned the Sands from my management consulting days. Therefore, I called the Ramada Inn in Weehawken and said in a demanding voice "Tina Sinatra please." To my surprise I was put right through to her suite. The phone rang twice and Tina answered the phone. I told her I had been waiting for her at Lepore's with the negatives, and then she laughingly told me she was lost in Hoboken. She told me to meet her at the Hoboken Path Station, on Monday where she would be completing the TV movie, "Sinatra." There I would give her the negatives and my idea about "Sinatra's From Here to Eternity."

When we met 8:00 a.m. Monday, she was terse but thankful and gave me her number in California for future correspondence. Our meeting was brief but, in my view, successful. I did not give Tina all the negatives because my goal was to meet Sinatra. Tina flew off to California with the negatives and the concept, "Sinatra's From Here to Eternity." Sid Mark's comments, "No one gets to Sinatra, not even the President," made me more determined to succeed. Through my research I was able to ascertain a direct number of a key Assistant to the President of Sinatra Enterprises. I knew that my message to Dorothy would have to have instant impact and credibility when she received my phone call in California. My plan was to inform her of the negatives and my meeting with Tina Sinatra as well as letting her know I and Mario Lepore would be at The Sands in Atlantic City during Mr. Sinatra's Performances. I knew telling her about Sinatra's "From Here to Eternity" would meet with instant rejection since the idea, in my judgement, was to overwhelming by phone, especially from someone she had never met before. When I called Sinatra Enterprises, the phone was answered by Dorothy. I asked for her by name and instantly, she started the screening inquisition. When I mentioned my meeting with Tina and the negatives of Frank in Hoboken, her entire demeanor changed to genuine politeness and concern. When I told her I would be at both performances at the Sands in July, she told me she was going to be there as well and we could meet. At the Sands I would present her with my Aunt's collection as well as my idea of "Sinatra's From Here to Eternity." In the back of my mind, of course, I was hoping that she might be accompanied by Ol' Blue Eyes himself. Sid Mark's comment, "Nobody gets to Sinatra," had left an indelible mark in my mind." I

was determined to meet the kid from Hoboken to get a yes or no
from the man himself on building his tribute as well as knowing
that a hotel would provide Hoboken with jobs, pride and the
recognition it deserves.

We arrived Wednesday evening, which was the night before
Mr. Sinatra was to perform. At 8:30, Mr. Lepore and I were having
a cocktail outside of the Restaurant, I'Medici at the Sands. As I was
going to the box office to get our tickets, Frank Sinatra and his
regal entourage passed by me on the way to I'Medici. I wasn't
aware of this until I returned to join Mario Lepore. Mr. Lepore
replied excitedly, "Did you see him? Did you see Sinatra?" I said,
"No. Where?" Mario continued, "he walked right by you with his
staff. He went to dinner at I'Medici." I instantly ran across the
hall and made reservation for dinner. I asked the Maitre 'de for a
table in the same room as Sinatra and explained that I had a
meeting with Dorothy in the morning concerning a collection of
priceless negatives for the Sinatra Estate.

We were immediately escorted into the Dining Room and
placed just below the dais where all the dignitaries including Frank
Sinatra were sitting. There were 15 people seated in the Royal
Box, which included his wife Barbara as well as his assistant,
Dorothy. Frank Sinatra Junior would enter about a half hour later.
Sinatra sat with his back facing the lower level of tables, which I
assumed was intentional not to be recognized by the public. He
sipped a glass of red wine and said nothing—while his staff
gregariously spoke in a low key, festive fashion. Dorothy sat at his
right hand side speaking quietly to him, and Mr. Sinatra just
nodded in agreement seeming very subdued and not interested in
any form of conversation.

From the back and the side profile of Mr. Sinatra, he looked
like a man soon to be 77 years of age. That youthful pal Joey
presence was gone, and he appeared to be well in the autumn of his
years. Frank Jr., who would be conducting a magnificent orchestra
at his Dad's performance, then entered the room. Frank Jr. quietly
sat by himself in the corner of the long table since the dinner had

begun without him. He was then being coaxed to sit closer with the members of the Royal Box. Barbara replied, "Come on Frankie, sit with us." He continued to stare down at his menu until suddenly we heard: "Come on, Don't be a schmuck." It was Francis Albert Sinatra advising his child of 48 years of age to join the group. Frank Jr. moved closer and the banquet had begun. Mr. Lepore and I were the only other members in the room sitting at a table below and felt honored that we were so close to the singing legend. Sinatra then began to join in the conversation in a low key manner. After dinner he was served a generous drink of Jack Daniels on the rocks. When he finished his drink, he rose from the table and proceeded down the dais and sat by himself across the way from me and Mr. Lepore. Six members of his staff moved down from the dais to join him. Sinatra began to speak and a quiet calm came over the room. He stared mystically into space reminiscing about Dean Martin, Sammy Davis, Jr. and great songwriters. He lit up a Camel cigarette and another Jack Daniels on the rocks was brought to him by the waiter. He spoke about Doris Day and said what a challenge she was to work with. He told how Sammy Davis Jr. "gave everything" away. He told us how he constantly calls Dean Martin, who refuses to come out of his house. He spoke about music, life and wisdom. Because his stories were so interesting, no one said a word when Mr. Sinatra spoke. It seemed like a ritual that members of the Royal Box be present on the night before his opening performance. As he continued to speak, he appeared to grow younger before our eyes and more vibrant with each sentence.

I became more at ease as Ol' Blue Eyes directed his conversation toward me and Mr. Lepore as he sensed how keenly we were listening to him. There we sat with the greatest entertainer in the world, just 3 kids from Hoboken: Mario, Ed and Francis Albert Sinatra. When his staff left the restaurant, Mr. Sinatra began to speak to me and Mario. Extemporaneously, from nowhere the words came, "you know" he replied in a humble and proud manner, if this can be possible, "I'm from the streets of Hoboken.

That's where I come from. That's where I was born. I'm just a regular guy born in a small city." I felt my chance had come. I raised myself from the chair and attempted to sit right next to Sinatra. I moved forward and Frank just looked at me and said nothing as if he welcomed someone's company who had been listening to him for the last 30 minutes. Immediately, two members from his security guard dashed from out of nowhere and ordered me back to my table. Frank was advised that they should leave, and we were told to wait until Mr. Sinatra left the restaurant. At this time I sensed he was a prisoner of his own success as he slowly walked away.

As Mr. Sinatra mystically left the room, I became very angry with myself thinking I was the cause for his abrupt exit. I thought if I only had waited instead of trying to inch closer to him, I might have succeeded in telling him about my idea of a hotel in his honor located on the very site where the first organized baseball game was played. I thought it mysteriously strange that he spoke to Mario and me about Hoboken. Ironically, we were trying to honor him, but as I reached out to him he was escorted from the room by his body guards. Although we reached Sinatra, we only listened while he spoke and could say nothing in return. I wondered if my vision was just a dream that almost became a reality.

You may be curious to know why Hoboken and Mr. Sinatra are very much a part of each other, but yet many miles away. I hope in some way that "Our Way" brings him close to us once again. For now I can only tell you why Hoboken and Mr. Sinatra are so much a part of each other. Hoboken is rich in history and tradition and is an extremely colorful town with a distinct personality. Mr. Sinatra possesses very similar qualities in his make up that has made him the greatest performer in the world. I can best describe Hoboken in a poem written by Mr. Jim Slade, which I discovered in the book "The Hoboken of Yesterday." Mr. Slade ends his beautiful poem with Henry Hudson sailing up the Hudson River, and I conclude with four lines dedicated to Mr. Sinatra.

HOBOKEN by Jim Slade
From: This Hoboken of Yesterday

On a head land bound by ridges
close along a river's shore,
Is a city filled with workers
And with plants some forty score.
The production is abundant
of the things that measure par,
In the wishes of great markets
whether near or scattered far.

By deep tunnel and broad turnpike
goods are speeded up the way,
While from rails and from dockside
cargo moves off night and day.
Sturdy freighter, stately liner
and the winged ships of the air.
Load and unload trusted products
made or brought by people there.

Its a very busy city
firmly built on one square mile
Where the red men once had traded
and the Dutch had owned a while.
English fought there with the natives
and a landlord served his king.
Then a state had taken over
with a bell of freedom's ring.
There was launched a steamboat ferry
first of all upon the sea,
And a Stevens schooled a castle
where is taught of things to be.
Claimed by baseball as a birthplace
of the teams with paying fare,

Home of Foster and a love song
to his wife with light brown hair.

Henry Hudson logged the writing
of a future he could see,
Later years were troops embarked there
to end war and set men free.
Now its heart for the world-wide commerce
still a challenge to bold men.
Treasure trove of growing promise
those of "vision" see again.[5]

One of "vision" was a young man
Who tried to make it on his own.
He left our town for stardom
And Hoboken was his home.

The following morning we met with Dorothy on the 19th floor at the Sand's Executive Suite. I brought many negatives and pictures of Mr. Sinatra from my Aunt's estate as well as my proposal on "Sinatra's From Here to Eternity." After going through two security checks, Mr. Lepore and I were brought to the Executive Suite and introduced to Dorothy. She was extremely polite and cordial and told us how Mr. Sinatra would take her to Hoboken and show her where he was born. "He would take me and show me the school he went to and would drive me to his home on Monroe Street and proudly show me the Arch on the building." She then asked me if the arch was still there, but then shifted her conversation to the pictures and negatives. She seemed extremely impressed with the collection and told us that she would send them off to Tina since I had told her that Tina would be expecting them from our meeting in Hoboken when she was filming the TV movie, "Sinatra." We were there almost 30 minutes talking about the pictures while the phone kept ringing constantly. Finally, I presented her with my proposal on Sinatra's "From Here to Eternity." She seemed shocked and confused about the idea. She told me that we could not use Sinatras name since it is copyright, plus we would be defrauding the public as it would not really be his hotel. I tried to explain that the hotel would be in his honor, and it would not cost Sinatra Enterprises a penny and it would also create badly needed jobs in Hoboken. People from around the world would come to this magnificent hotel. I could not believe that Dorothy had just finished telling me that Mr. Sinatra was so proud of the house in which he was born with a small arch over the entrance on Monroe Street. How would he feel if the world were coming to a Sinatra theater for the performing arts in his hotel with a fitting tribute to Baseball in a separate wing? She then told me that Mr. Sinatra would be flying on to Monaco for a two week vacation after his final performance at the Sands. She told me she would be submitting my proposal to Mr. Sinatra's lawyers, and we would be hearing from them within a month. I called her on two occasions but received no reply. My optimism began to fade on how Mr. Sinatra could return in triumph helping a city to rebound and grow and prosper with a hotel in his name. Till we meet again, Dorothy.

We attended Mr. Sinatra's performances both on Thursday and Friday evenings and had front row seats. Almost 30 years ago I had seen Judy Garland open the Felt Forum in Madison Square Garden and had never seen a greater performer. At almost 77 years of age, Mr. Sinatra's performance equaled Miss Garland. As he concluded with the song, "New York, New York," singing like the maestro he still is, the audience rose to their feet accompanied by a crescendo of applause. As he bowed graciously to his zealous supporters young and old, he walked toward me and Mr. Lepore, as we sat in the front row. He gazed directly at us with his blue eyes flashing just as he did at the Restaurant I'Medici, two nights before as if to say: "Thanks kids for listening to me when I told you I'm just a kid from the streets of Hoboken. These people listen to my songs, but you listened to my inner most thoughts—my story of where I was born." He bowed mystically and left the stage.

I will never forget that moment as long as I live, and I truly believe that if I had been able to speak at I Medici, I would have said, Mr. Sinatra: "We have come from your city to build you a hotel in your honor. We will place that small arch that you are so proud of from your home on downtown Monroe Street upon your new hotel. It's the very place you sat on the pier when you were a boy before Maxwell House was even built. It's On the Waterfront; it's Elysian Fields where the first Baseball game was played; it's Sinatra Drive. I feel at that moment Mr. Sinatra would have said, "Sure kid, as long as you do it My Way."

OLD HOBOKEN
"A Time That Was"

When Mario, Frank and me met at I'Medici, I sensed Mr. Sinatra remembered Hoboken the way it was in this picture, especially when he said, "I'm from Hoboken."

ARCHIE AND "PUNCH" PFLUG'S PLUMBING STORE ON 105 ADAMS STREET
(From the Galante collection)

Young Frank Sinatra poses in front of Grandfather "Punch" Pflug's plumbing store on Adams St. in Hoboken.

When he feels in his heart where life's destiny leads him
He knows what he has to do.

CHAPTER 4

Mayor Ed or Crazy Eddie

Three months before Mario, Frank, and me met at I'Medici, I experienced a horrifying evening which I will never forget, just as I remember the tragic date of November 22, 1963. When the President was assassinated, it was as if the world had stopped. When it began to evolve again, our country had changed radically. A time that was which focused on hope, progress, and sacrifice became a time of violence, uncertainty, and despair.

On April 7, 1992, I was arrested by the Deal Police just one mile from my home in Asbury Park, which severely damaged my candidacy for Mayor as well as Sinatra's "From Here to Eternity." Although I would not meet Mr. Sinatra until July, I believed our encounter would take place but had no idea how it would happen. April 7th was to be one of the most productive days of my life. In the afternoon I held the first baseball practice for our 14 and 15 year old Babe Ruth team. At the time I was managing Mr. Chuck Guy and Lost Weekend, and had scheduled an important meeting with Richard Brant, Director of Entertainment and Mr. Mark Joliani Vice President of The Long Branch Hilton to consummate a contract in the groups behalf. I was also trying to assist Carlos, a young man who had an immigration problem, as well as find him suitable employment with the Hilton. The major reason, however, was to obtain the necessary financial backing for a hotel on the Hudson in Mr. Sinatra's honor. Finally, that evening I would be off to McCloons Rum Runner to ask Mr. Bruce Foster to perform at my Mayoral campaign kick off dinner, which was just a few months away.

In spite of the financial collapse of my real estate investments, I was emotionally up beat because I believed so deeply that Sinatra's "From Here to Eternity" would become a reality. In the evening Mr. Lepore was to meet me home in Asbury Park, and we were to have dinner with Mr. Brant and Carlos after our meeting at the Hilton. Richard Brant told me he was looking for hard working individuals with managerial potential. I immediately recommended Carlos since I knew him as a bartender at The Brass Rail in Hoboken. By now if you are thinking Hoboken sure has a lot of bars, I assure you, you're right. During the war Hoboken was referred to as The Barbary Coast because of the many bars in the city, but today it is more like Bourbon Street in New Orleans, being so rich in culture.

Richard Brant liked the proposal on the band and also felt Carlos might fit well at the Hilton. He also loved the delicious Italian meal Mario cooked for him and was fascinated by the pictures I gave him of Mr. Sinatra. He thought my candidacy for Mayor was impressive and exciting, but when I told him of my idea of Sinatra's "From Here to Eternity" he looked at me in awe and disbelief and exclaimed, "Eddie, all I want to do is run this hotel. You run for Mayor. But a Hilton in Hoboken. You're way out there, Eddie."

After dinner I drove him to Rumson to a beautiful Restaurant called the Fisherman's Wharf. Mr. Brant was looking to buy a restaurant on his own, and he told me if I could find such a place that perhaps there would be some opportunity in ownership for me and Mr. Lepore. What he meant was: You and Mario work the business, and I will get the necessary backers. When I brought him to the restaurant, he loved the site immediately. He told me he would be calling his backers would proceed with an offer since I had already ascertained a price from the existing owner.

With the strict enforcement of (DWI) driving while intoxicated, many bars and restaurants were losing up to 50% of their revenue. Entertainers who worked 5 days a week found themselves reduced to 2 days a week if they were lucky. This was a major reason why Jim Reardon went west. I drove with Richard Brant back to the Hilton in Long Branch, and we agreed to draw up a contract for the band Chuck Guy and Lost Weekend.

I was then off to Tim McCloon's Rum Runner in Monmouth to meet with Bruce Stephen Foster, the man who was to co-write Hoboken's Tribute song, "A Time That Was" in honor of Mr. Frank Sinatra. Although Chuck Guy and Lost Weekend was to perform in Hoboken to officially kick off my campaign for Mayor in June, I wanted Bruce to sing at Hoboken's posh supper club Frankie and Johnnies, On The Waterfront, the same bar where "On The Waterfront" was filmed starring Marlon Brando and Eva Marie Saint. Since I frequently went to see Bruce perform, he accepted my request to perform in October as the Mayoral election would then be only four months away. I made certain that I would drink no more than 2 wine spritzers for the entire evening, since the day carried a great potential for many people. At 11:30, Bruce asked me to sing a Sinatra song with him. Since I know almost every song Mr. Sinatra has recorded by heart, I decided to sing my favorite from Pal Joey, "Bewitched, Bothered and Bewildered." After singing I felt so fulfilled that things went so well during the course of the day and told Bruce I would call him shortly. I left McCloons and got into my Chrysler, New Yorker, with Carlos while Mr. Lepore drove the candy truck back to Asbury Park.

When I left McCloons Restaurant, I proceeded on Ocean Avenue. I was about one mile from my home in Asbury Park when I saw flashing lights in my rear view mirror. I couldn't believe I was being stopped by the Deal Police. I became very fearful as the officer approached my car, and my heart began beating rapidly thinking I would be immediately tested for Driving While Intoxicated. I started to get out of the car to ask the officer what was wrong. He screamed, "Stay in the car!" as if he was making a drug raid on a tip off he had received. Again he screamed, "I told you to stay in the car!" As he approached me, he shined a flashlight in my eyes screaming at the same time: "I want to see your license and registration." I told him that my license was in the attache case which was in the trunk of the car. I fumbled for the insurance and the registration in the glove compartment. He then ordered me out of the car and told me to come around the back by the trunk of the car. He began screaming, "Open the trunk, hurry up, open the trunk!" When I opened the trunk, I unlocked my briefcase and nervously searched through its contents trying to find my driver's license. During this time credit cards began dropping out of my wallet and he began shouting, "I said your license, not your credit cards." Finally, I showed him my license.

During this time he had ordered Carlos to stay in the passenger's seat. He then began his three hour torture. I first had to walk a straight line and then hold my one leg in the air counting backwards to thirty three. This is hard enough for an athlete to perform let alone a shocked victim pulled from a car not knowing the real reason. Next I had to recite the alphabet and finally perform a finger to nose exercise that no one could comprehend, especially if you're sober. After the final test, I felt confident that I would be allowed to continue home. He then shined a pinlight into my eyes warning me not to move. After that he told me to turn around, and informed me that I was under arrest for DWI. As the steel cuffs wrenched tightly around my wrists, I recalled what Barbara Yeger had potentiously said when I showed her the Sinatra photos just three weeks ago. "Let's hope those pictures aren't a curse, Eddie." Almost in shock, I turned my neck nervously as the officer screamed loudly in a demonic tone, "What are you doing, resisting arrest?" Officer Galen Lowery pushed me into his squad car and laid me down in the back. He already had my keys and ordered Carlos to go with another officer named Estelle. They began searching my car, starting first with the trunk. He then came back screaming in a violent manner: "How do you open the door of the car," while dangling 20 keys in front of my face in obscure darkness. I responded, "How can I show you the key when I can't see in the dark with my hands tied behind my back?" He ran back to the car and finally managed to open the car door. He then came back with his partner. I was calling him from the squad car to let him know that the lock was difficult to open. I then remembered crying out, "Oh God, help me." He returned with his buddy Sergeant Estelle. My fear turned to anger, now knowing what they were doing. They began shouting in the car, "Where were you coming from?" The worst thing I could have done was to tell them the truth. I told them I was coming from McCloons Rum Runner and spoke with Bruce Foster to ask him to perform at my Mayoral Campaign rally. Before I could say anything further, both officers broke into laughter and began their mocking, "Hi Mayor. Hey this is the Mayor of Hoboken." "He don't look like the Mayor to me," replied Officer Estelle as he started to laugh. I was then brought in handcuffs to the Deal Police Station. I was praying that they didn't discover the Sinatra photos which I had in the trunk of my car because now I sensed real danger.

When they brought me to the interrogation room, they began filming me on tape for about ten seconds as one officer held my head ordering me to stare into the camera. After the first ordeal, Officer Estelle removed the camera and Officer Lowery's demeanor changed. I had no way of knowing for certain, but I just sensed there was a hidden camera. Lowery now politely asked me: "Would you like to do your psycho-physical skill tests again?" Arrogantly, I snapped back, asking, "What's that?" "You know," he replied in a gentlemanly fashion, "The exercises we did outside." "Oh, you mean where going to do that again," I commented. Oh, OK! You're the judge. Anything you want me to do, I'll do." He replied politely: "I'm not the judge sir." He then went to his desk for his personal camera, and the DWI audition began. As I performed all the tests in near perfect fashion, there was one episode almost comical in the taping. Lowery began having trouble with his camera trying to focus in on me. I actually asked him if he was ready for his next scene as if we were making a movie. He responded, preoccupied with technical difficulties, "No, not yet." He then looked up from under his camera and said, "OK, start walking." When I began preparing for my trial, I researched the DWI laws and discovered if I refused the psycho-physical skill test on camera, I would automatically be convicted. I then knew why his demeanor changed from Gestapo agent to an Army Chaplin when we began making the movie.

The video tape ran almost an hour and I continued to ask him: "If the judge views the tape in court, and finds me innocent on tape, would the breatholizer refusal negate the DWI charge?" I was trying to get an answer from him since the document he placed before me to read made no sense. It was written in a legal form to obviously confuse the apprehended about your rights as it related to DWI. As he was preparing the breatholizer, he refused to respond to my question. I was in the interrogation room for almost two hours now fighting mad pushing him and two other patrolmen to the brink of beating me. I had reached the point where I didn't care about the consequences because I knew I was a victim of a set up. Lowery then began to get irritated with me questioning him and said, "Now I'm asking you one time, are you going to take the breatholizer or not?" Once again I asked him, "If the judge reviews the tape and finds me innocent performing the tests, will this negate the refusal to take the breatholizer?" He finally gave in and replied, "Yes." I then replied tersely, "Then no, I won't take the breath test." That's all he needed because now he had his man.

Without any further hesitation, he proceeded to write me out the first ticket, which was for DWI. The second ticket was for refusal to take a breatholizer. Before he handed me the second summons, I always thought DWI and refusal were all inclusive meaning if you're drunk, you're drunk. From the ordeal I learned they were two separate offenses. Lowery, through his demonic cunning, was able to hit the jack pot for Deal—meaning double revenue. As he began to write out the third ticket, he looked up smiling diabolically and said: "Do you know the real reason I stopped you?" In a daze, I replied, "No," but grossly intent on knowing why. He again smiled diabolically and said, "You're headlight was out. When you pulled out all those gold fancy credit cards from your wallet, I decided to bust you. I was gonna let you go, but I don't like guys like you."

A third officer, who was the radio dispatcher at the scene of my arrest, then gave me back my attache case, and I was relieved to find that everything was in tact, especially the Sinatra photos and my proposal on Sinatra's "From Here to Eternity." I never felt so broken in my life and would never regain my vitality until Mario, Frank and me met at I'Medici three months later. In a state of abject depression, I called Mario from the interrogation room to let him know of our strange disappearance while Carlos was vomiting profusely in the lavatory from the stressful episode. At 3:30 am, Mario drove to the Deal Police Department, and we were finally home.

The following day I asked Carlos to be a witness in my behalf, and he assured me that he would testify. However, when I went to see him that Friday at The Brass Rail, where he was bartending, his attitude had changed. I sensed he was anxious about his immigration problem. I told him I had gotten a copy of the DWI video, and it showed beyond a reasonable doubt that I was not under the influence of alcohol. When he appeared to be disinterested, our meeting almost ended in a physical altercation. I left Carlos now knowing I was without a witness but felt extremely confident of my innocence especially when I discovered the video tape had been edited to persecute. Just one week later I received a reply from Congressman Guarini in Carlos' behalf that read:

Dear Mr. Shirak:
*　　Thank you for contacting my Jersey City district office*
regarding a friend of yours, Mr. Carlos Medina, who has

been experiencing difficulties with the Immigration and
Naturalization Service. In order to be of some assistance, I
have contacted the proper authorities on Mr. Carlos Medina
behalf, and I will keep him abreast of any correspondence
pertaining to this matter. I appreciate your bringing this
matter to my attention. I will make every effort to resolve
this issue for Mr. Carlos Medina. With regards, I am
                        Sincerely,
                        FRANK J. GUARINI
                        Member of Congress
                        BUY AMERICAN!

On April 9th, I retained the services of my first DWI lawyer.
Since my court date was April 13, I now had to devote all my
energies to my defense. I spent about a half hour with him, and he
told me that he thought I had an excellent case, which made me
feel much better mentally. He then asked for a $900.00 check to
represent me and told me he had to "write for discovery," which
dazzled me with his legal expertise at the time. I found out later,
that I could have written for discovery for $15.00, but at the time I
was confused and ignorant in regard to DWI. When I called him
on Friday, I was told by his secretary that he left for a weekend to
Disney World with his family. On Monday I anxiously called
him, since this was the day I was to be tried. He then had my case
rescheduled at the Municipal Court in Deal. I decided I did
not want a lawyer from Disney World and retained one from
Asbury Park, who supposedly knew the court system better in
Deal. When I called my first lawyer, he was shocked why I no
longer wanted him to represent me. He told me that he had
already done the bulk of the work meaning writing a letter for
discovery. He kept $500.00 for his services, which I'm sure paid
his fare to Disney World.

When the second lawyer viewed the tape with me at the Deal
Police Department, I saw that the tape had been edited. I saw one
second pauses in the tape and thought I could build a case on

tampering with evidence. As I saw the breaks in the tape, I shouted: "Dick, they cut the tape. They cut the tape!" This didn't seem to phase the counselor, but he was impressed with how well I performed on the tape. He said, "Ed, you weren't drunk at all. You performed in near perfect fashion. Why didn't you take the breath test?" I said, "Dick, when you go through such a trying ordeal, you lose your trust in any form of justice." Since I wanted a lawyer who would prove my innocence on the edited tape issue, I sought further counsel. In all I spoke with six DWI lawyers. One lawyer did not accept a consultation fee but suggested I seek psychiatric help since he would not believe my meeting with the Governor on Baseball Day as well as my idea of a Hotel on the Hudson honoring Mr. Sinatra. This guy was supposed to be one of the greatest defense lawyers around for DWI. He told me statistically that DWI offenses have a 98% conviction rate. In my mind this meant this guy never wins a case and makes thousands. He has a great job!

I hired a private investigator to check the business practices on the company where the tapes were prepared. The agency charged me $500.00 for their investigation of the video store where the police jobbed out the DWI tapes. I became suspicious of the company when they told me they could work "magic" with their cameras meaning they could make anything viewed on tape disappear before the naked eye with their sophisticated equipment. Because I was so convinced that the tape had been edited, I called Mr. Bob Bodziner, Senior Producer of The First Annual Baseball Day in June of 1990. He agreed to review the DWI tape along with his technical editor at Channel 9 headquarters The Phoenix Communication Group to see if any editing took place. Mr. Bodziner wrote the following letter to Brian Kennedy, Esq., the lawyer who I finally chose to represent me:

Dear Mr. Kennedy,
 On June 3, 1992, I viewed the D.W.I tape of Ed
Shirak. The tape was approximately 17 minutes long, and

*in my opinion there were no edits within that time frame.
One big inconsistency I picked out was with respect to the
time of day as stated by the police officer on the tape. After
Mr. Shirak signed his Miranda rights, the officer looked at
his watch and clearly stated "2 A.M." Approximately 10
minutes later (give or take 15 seconds) the police officer once
again looked at his watch and clearly stated "2:52 A.M."
Perhaps the officer misread his watch or perhaps some
editing did take place, undetected by my trained eye.*

    *If you would like to discuss this matter any further ,
feel free to contact me at the address listed in the enclosed
business card.*

Very truly yours,
Bob Bodziner, Senior Producer

Because I remember vividly what went on in the interrogation room on the morning of April 8, I am certain, beyond a doubt, that the tape was edited to persecute. However, when I received my copy of the tape from the police department, the edits which I had clearly seen with my second lawyer were gone. It was magic!

I postponed my trial until after my kick-off campaign rally at Signore's Lounge on June 19, since I feared if I were found guilty, I would make my first speech with a criminal record. The irony of this terrible episode was that I was President of the Hoboken Babe Ruth League, which was initially run by the Police Athletic League. If I were elected mayor, I had promised to give half my salary to the Hoboken Police Department to stop bar disturbances in the city.

In Municipal Court in Deal, I was found guilty of both DWI and refusal to take a breatholizer, since the judge also viewed me being drunk on the tape. My lawyer convinced me to go with the defense of " A picture is worth a thousand words" since he believed that he had never seen anyone perform the tests on the DWI tape so perfectly. After being convicted, I appealed my case and was off to Superior Court in Freehold. During this time I learned you can not change your testimony when you appeal to a higher court. Therefore, my defense was once again, "a picture is worth a thousand words." When I was tried on Jan. 2, 1993, the hanging judge was not impressed. I also had a young Afro American prosecuting attorney trying me, and he was proving my innocence by his own ignorance of DWI. The hanging judge stopped him politely and put him back on track and convicted me.

Mario Lepore

The ten thousand dollars I spent to prove my innocence was the campaign monies I had set aside to run for Mayor. Here is how DWI serves as one of the greatest revenue pork barrels in the country: In DWI you have no right to a jury. It is only you, your lawyer, the cop, the prosecutor, and the judge. You have no right to remain silent when you are in custody for breath samples and no legal right to have an attorney, physician, or anyone else present for the purpose of taking breath samples. When convicted, you are committed to an Intoxicated Driver Resource Center IDRC for 12 to 48 hours with a cost of $200.00. When you attend your first day at the center, they determine if you should be placed in an alcoholic rehabilitation group AA by a psychological test they administer to you. This is for first offenders! If you do not attend the further assigned punishment, your license is revoked again. I was fortunate that my testing indicated that I did not have to go for further treatment. I will never forget that terrible evening when Galen Lowery saw my headlight out as I drove through Deal bewitched, bothered and bewildered.

I am now on bicycle campaigning with my slogan, "The People Must Be Served." I am running for Mayor with no campaign funds, financially bankrupt and building Sinatra's "From Here to Eternity" without having met the great star to tell him of his tribute. Although I still believed I would meet Sinatra because miracles do happen when you have faith, I began to feel I was Crazy Eddie not Mayor Ed. When Governor Florio came to Hoboken campaigning for his re-election, I personally gave him the following letter since I still believed so deeply in the tribute to Mr. Frank Sinatra.

> *Dear Governor Florio:*
> *I very much appreciated the time you took from your busy schedule to read my petition regarding The Sinatra On The Waterfront Hotel in Hoboken New Jersey. I will be going to trial on an alleged DWI charge on July 6 in Deal, New Jersey, as you are aware of. I will prove that day that*

the video tape the Deal Police took of me was edited. If I am found guilty, I will take my case to the highest court since the Rights of Man are being seriously violated. After my meeting on July 22nd and 23rd with respective key members on the Sinatra staff at the Sands Hotel in Atlantic City, I will inform you of the outcome since you are aware of my meetings with Tina Sinatra. Thanks again sir for your interest in this matter. I will formally announcing my candidacy for Mayor on Baseball Day June 19 as I indicated to you in my last letter. It was a pleasure meeting you and presenting you with a Hoboken Mug of Lepore's Chocolate. I felt very proud that you remembered BASEBALL DAY and the song we produced, "Baseball was Born in this town."

> *Sincerely,*
> *Ed Shirak Jr.*
> *Candidate for Mayor*
> *City of Hoboken 1993*

Although I did not receive a personal reply from the Governor, I sensed he still remembered Baseball Day since the following letters arrived quick and courteous from his Directors.

Dear Mr. Shirak:

Please excuse me for not responding sooner, however, on behalf of Governor Florio, I'd like to express my sincere thanks for your recent letter requesting him to attend your 1992 Baseball Day Event on June 19, 1992. The Governor regrets that he was unable to join you, but his time had already been fully committed.

Although his schedule did not permit him to share this occasion with you, I hope he may have the opportunity again in the future.

Please know your understanding is greatly appreciated.

> *Very truly yours,*
> *Margaret A. Young*
> *Director of Scheduling*

Dear Mr. Shirak:
Thank you for your letter to Governor Florio.
While the Governor certainly appreciates the
confidence you have placed in his ability to assist you, the
constitutional separation of powers prevents him from
intervening in the judicial process. I can only suggest that
you continue pursuing this matter with the court in the
county where the incident you mentioned took place.
    Again, thank you for taking the time to contact
Governor Florio.

               Sincerely,
               Viola Foster
               Director
               Office of Constituent Relations

One month before Mario Lepore and I came face to face with Francis Albert Sinatra, I announced my candidacy for Mayor of the City of Hoboken. It was once again Baseball Day in Hoboken, and Lepore's had won the Babe Ruth City Championship for the second consecutive year. In the evening I held my campaign kick-off rally at Signore's lounge, which was previously known as the Continental. Mr. Sinatra tried, on many occasions, to sing at the Old Continental Hotel, just across the street, but was rejected because the owner felt he had no talent. Mr. Frank Totaro, who still bartends in Hoboken, told me this story and will tell you later of his encounter with Mr. Sinatra and his memories of his mother Dolly.

    June 19th was also the same day that Jim Reardon talked himself out of the psychiatric hospital for one day to come to Hoboken to sing "Baseball was Born in this Town." Steven Speiser, the head of the American Baseball Heritage Society, was still in control of Baseball Day. With deep compassion, he told me: "This guy better not crack up on me Ed when he sings the song. There are a lot of important people on hand." Impressed with his genuine concern for Jim's condition, I replied, "Don't worry Steve, Jimmy is a pro. He don't crack." As Jim began to sing to the audience, he began to regain the vitality he once had and began enjoying life again. After Jim performed without cracking, we stopped at Trapani's for pizza, the same tavern where he sang over one year ago, when he was healthy and brimming with pride. After we finished eating, Jim was driven back to the hospital but recovered remarkably after Baseball Day. He was released within one week and began a productive life once again.

The same evening for the Mayoral kick-off campaign entertainment, I hired Mr. Chuck Guy and Lost Weekend to perform at Signore's Lounge. At 17, Chuck began singing in Florida with the Miami Kids and performed for the Nixon children as well as the Nixon's at the West Palm Beach Hotel. He was the lead singer for the famous party band Salvation, who performed in New Jersey for more than 12 years. In the 70's baby boomers came throughout the tri state area to see Salvation. Occasionally, Bruce Springstein would go to The Osprey Hotel in Manasquan to see Chuck perform since Bruce was just beginning his career singing at The Stone Pony in Asbury Park, New Jersey. When you ask Chuck about Mr. Springstein's visits to The Osprey, he smiles and says, "that's where he learned all his moves, watching me." You would be astounded how a man with such incredible talent never really made it to the top. He still performs every summer at The Osprey Hotel in Manasquan where baby boomers still come to see him. His wife, Lenore and his mother-in-law, Mary Cunningham, will be at his side.

In 1950 and 51, Mary Cunningham won the Gold and Silver medals for the United States Olympic Swim Team. She made no profit from her outstanding achievement because it was a time that was when life's values stressed honor and integrity above wealth. Mary, Chuck Guy, and his wife Lenore are extraordinary people and prophets in their own way-making people happy.

At my campaign kick off on June 19, Chuck rocked Signores but few people came to hear me speak. Only a small following of friends and relatives were present. All I could think of was, if Mr.

Sinatra was told he had no talent as a singer at the Continental Hotel, the people are probably giving me a similar message. Because my idea was so bizarre and unlikely to become a reality in the minds of many men and women, Hudson Current wrote a front page story on the vision I had on November 22, 1992, four months before the election.

On May 11, 1993, I ran for Mayor of Hoboken in a field of eight receiving 77 votes. We had 6 debates, and I feel I had won them all having $1,000 to spend on my campaign against $650,000 collectively against the other candidates. Over the last 40 years, all of Hoboken's Mayors have been Italian because of a very special person you will know of shortly in "Our Way." Pope John Paul II has reigned for 18 years and is the first Pope that has not been Italian in 500 years. As we enter into the third millennium, perhaps Hoboken will see fit to elect a Polish Mayor if I so choose to run again.

November 1992

Pursuing Sinatra "From Here to Eternity"

Hoboken businessman wants to turn Maxwell House into a hotel

By David Cogswell, *Reporter staff writer*

Ed Shirak is a man with a dream. He wants to turn Maxwell House into a luxury hotel and name it after Frank Sinatra.

Shirak is a partner in Lepore's Chocolate at Sixth and Garden Streets and plans to be a candidate for mayor of Hoboken in 1993. In his mother's basement, he discovered a handful of rare photographs of Frank Sinatra which had belonged to his deceased uncle, a lithographer. One in particular caught his eye, a picture of a very intense looking 17-year-old Sinatra sitting barefoot, cross-legged on a boardwalk staring across the Hudson. Shirak says the photo was taken at a lumberyard at the site of what later became Maxwell House along River Road, now officially renamed Frank Sinatra Drive.

The vision

Jogging along the Hudson one day, Shirak had a vision of the Maxwell House factory converted into a colossal luxury hotel called "Sinatra's From Here to Eternity."

"People were looking at the Maxwell House sign and saying 'What are we going to do with it?'" he says. "The facility was intact, with plumbing, electricity, office space and parking. It could mean renewed tax revenue for our city, as well as jobs for our people. Finally Hoboken could give Mr. Sinatra a long-awaited tribute, his crowning jewel on the Hudson."

Once the idea took root in Shirak's mind, it began to grow. Soon it included a Baseball Hall of Fame within the hotel. He began making phone calls to people he thought could help make his idea a reality. He sought financial backing from General Foods, Philip Morris, Hilton International and others.

Through Maurice Fitzgibbons, he contacted Governor Florio and presented the proposal to him. Florio directed Shirak to the Economic Development Agency. All along the way, Shirak received interest in measured tones, but nothing could really happen without the approval of the man whose name was to be used, and making contact with Sinatra was not as easy as contacting a mere governor or the head of a large corporation.

Fate steps in

Shirak was aided by fate in his attempt to contact Sinatra when the head cameraman of the production crew for Tina Sinatra's miniseries "Sinatra" came into his store at Sixth and Garden Streets. The cameraman was so taken by the photos of Sinatra hanging over the cash register, that he offered to introduce Shirak to Tina Sinatra, who was nearby filming the TV movie of her father's life. This led to an encounter with Tina Sinatra, but still no meeting with Frank, and no permission to use the name.

Shirak was relentless. He contacted Sinatra Enterprises and spoke to an assistant to the president named Dorothy. She let down her screen a little when Shirak told of his contact with Tina Sinatra. Armed with his booty of Sinatra negatives, Shirak was able to arrange a tentative meeting with Dorothy during the time Sinatra would be in Atlantic City to perform at the Sands Hotel in July.

On to the Sands

Shirak and his partner Lepore had tickets to both of Sinatra's performances at the Sands. They arrived in Atlantic City the night before the performances. Once again his persistence was aided by chance. Standing outside the I Medici Restaurant, Lepore saw Sinatra and his entourage going into the restaurant.

With some fast talking and a big tip, Shirak managed to get a table in the same room as the Sinatra group. From there, Shirak watched in rapt attention as his 76-year-old hero reminisced at dinner with intimates who paid little attention.

Finally, all six members of the entourage left the room, with Sinatra still talking, now directing his stories to Lepore and Shirak, the only ones left in the room. Shirak rose to get closer and was immediately accosted by security guards who, he said, "dashed out of nowhere" and told him to leave. Oh well.

The next day Shirak had his meeting with Dorothy, the assistant to the president of Sinatra Enterprises. She was happy to receive the photos of Sinatra b ut when Shirak told her of his plan for a hotel, she "seemed shocked and confused." The conversation ended with Dorothy telling Shirak she would submit his proposal to the lawyers and he would hear a reply "within a month." No such reply has materialized, however, and Ed Shirak says, "My optimism has begun to fade."

Mr. Sinatra, oh beneficent one, we await your response. ❑

There'll be times we long for and miss those days of old
The families, friends and memories and the love they always hold

CHAPTER 5

Dolly, Cookie and Maime were Just the Same

Marie Vieser (Shirak) was born in Poland. I mean Austria. No, it was Iowa. My grandmother was the greatest story teller I could ever remember. Cookie was her nickname, because she was one tough cookie. When we were children, Nana, as we called her, told us that she came to Hoboken in a barrel from Iowa, and it rolled down the hill from Jersey City, and it crashed and struck a huge tree. The barrel shattered in pieces and she landed in town, just about the same time Natalie, (Garavante), Sinatra arrived in Hoboken from Genoa, Italy. Maime or Mary (Gil) Pflug was born in Hoboken as was her husband Rudy ("Punch") Pflug. They called her Maime because her name was Mary, and because she had such fire and spark in a frame of just 95 pounds. She was a beautiful woman.

Nana Shirak spoke many dialects and languages. She was able to converse in Italian, Polish, German as well as Hebrew. She possessed tremendous charm, was very fun loving, and was also full of mischief. Everybody wanted to go to Nana's house because she played with the children just like she was one of the kids. Cookie was the backbone of the family, especially when my grandfather became ill with tuberculosis. I remember him only once when he was recovering from TB. He took me to the park at Elysian Fields in Hoboken where the first baseball game was played. He held my hand all the way, and then we returned to his home on eleventh and Washington Street. In about one week he was rushed to the hospital complaining of stomach pains. The doctor thought it was nothing serious. Contrary to his diagnosis, Grandpas appendix burst, which led to peritonitis, and he died unexpectedly at St. Mary Hospital in Hoboken. It was a great shock to the family at such a young age of 51, especially after overcoming tuberculosis.

Every Sunday our entire family would gather over Cookie's house for buns and coffee. My grandmother must have moved more than six times in Hoboken, and we always kidded her that she was just like a gypsy. The Shirak family actually lost their house in Willow terrace during the depression over back taxes of only $100. My grandfather did not believe in borrowing money so he let the city take the house. Cookie's home was like an open kitchen. She fed everyone in the family as well as anyone who needed a meal. I mean literally she fed everyone! When you went to Cookies house, you never knew whom you would meet. We would come to her house on 6th and Washington Street and always be surprised whom she was feeding along with her three cats, or sometimes four, or maybe five. I would walk into her apartment and be introduced to a new acquaintance on many occasions. Since I ran errands for my grandmother, I would ask her quietly in the parlor, as her guest was eating a delicious, home cooked Polish meal, "Nana, who is this person?" She would say sweetly; "Keep quiet you little son of a bee. He's hungry. He needs food. Don't embarrass me, you little son of a bitch bastard." Believe it or not, this was an expression of her affection for me. I would then reply, "Nana, you're always cursing!" She would then break into a saintly smile and say, "Oh, I'm sorry my darling Edward. I didn't mean it.

I'm so ashamed." This was my Grandmother. She was as tough as anyone but had the greatest compassion for anyone who needed to be helped whether it be food or money. Cookie could charm anyone by her genuine warmth. Because the family was her life, she raised five loving children. My uncles and aunts were very good to me because of the love and affection my grandmother showed them throughout her life. I was very lucky.

I always loved going to my grandmother's house because something exciting was always happening. Cookie cooked all day, cleaned all night and never slept. Because she was very ill with diabetes and severe heart trouble, she popped nitroglycerin pills like kids eat peanuts at a baseball game. My grandmother had angina attacks at least two to three times a day and would sit down and moan with pain that would frighten everyone in the house. The next minute, after ingesting two or three nitro pills, she was up and about laughing once again. At times I became so frightened especially when I was with her alone and would ask: "Nana, are you going to die?" She would gently hug me and say smilingly, "I'm not going to die, you little son of a bee. My darling Edward, "why are you always afraid?" Again, I would reply. "Nana, you're always cursing." She once again would smile and say. "Oh, I'm sorry, I'm so ashamed?"

Everyone knew Marie Vieser (Shirak) alias Cookie on Washington Street. She stopped and spoke to everyone. There was never enough time in the day for my grandmother. After all, she spoke five languages, and I know she never went past the fourth grade. She had an impeccable vocabulary along with the son of a bitch bastard repertoire if she had to make her point to people who understood no other language.

I remember when she used to cook for my brother Kenny and my two cousins Charlie and Carol Romano. We would sit in the parlor and wait for the fun to start. You see she kept all her pots in the oven and when she cooked she used every one since she was preparing food for at least 10 people a day, whether you were family or not. She would pull out one pot and then there would be a landslide of pots falling out of the oven and crashing on to the kitchen floor. Then you would hear Cookie screaming, "these son of a bitchin bastard pots. Get in their you son of a bitchin bastards." Then she would stop and you would hear. "Oh, my darling grandchildren, I'm so ashamed. Nana's sorry." By now we were almost in tears laughing since we knew the script by heart. She really made us laugh. I could write a novel on Cookie and how she always seemed interested in anyone who had a problem in spite of the battle she waged with heart disease for over 20 years. All I could say in her honor was that everybody knew Cookie and loved her for the compassion she showed for everyone she met.

In 1965 Cookie suffered a severe heart attack in Ocean Grove, New Jersey, vacationing with her family. She was taken back to St. Mary Hospital in Hoboken by my Uncle Jimmy Galante, where the vigil began for the next three days. The doctor told us that he didn't know what was keeping her alive. He told us that he had never seen a person with such a bad heart along with such a powerfully strong will to live. Finally, after three days of suffering, Aunt Kathleen (Ward) Shirak told us that Cookie had died. My aunt, who was a registered nurse, along with my mother, had been nursing my grandmother at the hospital. All fifteen members of the immediate family sat in silence when we received word. We all expected the final outcome but couldn't believe she was dead. Upon Cookie's passing, things immediately began to change. There were no more family Sunday meetings at her house, nor the battle of the pots, just as Don Quixote fought with Windmills. The stories and the adventures at Cookies were over. Marie Vieser (Shirak) was the nuts and bolts of family values and tradition. I sum up her life by a poem written by Corinne (Roosevelt) Robinson;

SOLDIER OF PAIN

Not in the trenches, torn by shot and shelling,
  Not on the plain,

Bombed by the foe; but calm and unrebelling,
  Soldier of Pain!

Facing each day, head high with gallant laughter,
  Anguish supreme;
What accolade in what divine hereafter
  Shall this redeem?

Through the long night of racked, recurrent waking,
  Till the long day,
Fraught with distress, brings but the same heartbreaking
  Front for the fray.

In a far land our Nation's patriots, willing,
  Fought, and now lie-
But you-as brave-a harder fate fulfilling,
  Dare not to die![3]

Mary (Gil) Pflug was born in Hoboken, New Jersey in 1888 and married Rudy Pflug in 1908. Maime, as she was known, raised eight brothers and sisters when she was a young girl and bore seven children of her own. My grandmother never went past the second grade at Our Lady of Grace Elementary School in Hoboken, because she had to work and help her mother with eight children. Maime taught herself to read, write and clean homes to make a living while raising my aunts and uncles. Because she was a strict disciplinarian, her children grew up with strong family values. She was an assiduous worker, an excellent cook and immaculately well kept, while her husband Rudy worked as a plumber in his own business on Adam Street in Hoboken. You can see in the photo section of "Our Way" a picture of Frank Sinatra when he was a boy standing outside of my grandfather's store on Adam Street.

On Saturday evening my grandfather used to go to Vic Lavari's bar, which was the only night he ever drank since his hours in the plumbing business were tough and very demanding. While at the bar, Rudy got into an argument with Charlie Seeger, a middle weight boxing contender at that time. This is not to be confused with Dolly Sinatra's younger brother Babe Seeger, who was an excellent boxer as well. During this time many Italian people changed their surnames to Irish and German to have a better chance of advancing themselves. As soon as Rudy Pflug and Charlie Seeger started fighting, my grandfather fired a solid right hand to Charlie Seeger's jaw and he went down. From then on he was known as Punch. A friend came over to my grandfather and said: "Rudy, do you know who you just knocked out?" My grandfather replied in a confused manner, "No." "It's Charlie Seeger! He is the contending middleweight boxer." "Well," Punch replied, "if he's a contending middleweight fighter, who the hell am I?" From then on he was known as Punch.

In 1918 my grandparents bought their first home on 814 Bloomfield Street. They paid $9,500, which was a lot of money at the time. Punch even bought a movie house downtown while still working hard as a plumber. Maime worked all sorts of jobs as a housekeeper while maintaining their beautiful house on Bloomfield Street. When my grandfather became gravely ill in 1939, my grandmother nursed him at home. He died at 53 years of age on New Years Eve, leaving five children and Maime. To this day we still don't know what the real cause of death was. My grandmother did everything she could to keep the house. She scrubbed floors and cooked for anyone just to save 814 Bloomfield Street. When she could no longer keep up with the financial demands of the property, she sold the house for $5,000. Maime was now poor. During this time, the Sinatras moved around the corner from the Pflug's on 841 Garden Street.

Although Maime began to drink heavily, she always stood up for her children. My mother told me that once she went out on a date with a gentlemen by the name of Jimmy Higgins, who lived in the same tenement building as my mother and grandmother on 913 Park Avenue. This was after my grandmother lost the house on Bloomfield Street. Jimmy drove my mother to Jersey City and made an advance at her. My mother told him that she wanted to go home. He slapped my mother in the face and told her to walk home from Jersey City. The next morning my mother came down to breakfast before work and had a black and blue mark on her face from the slap she had received from Mr. Higgins. My grandmother saw her bruised face and in her stern manner asked: "What happened?" My mother burst into tears and told her that Jimmy hit her. Maime was only five feet tall and weighed 95 pounds but had a temper that I have never seen the likes of in my life. I know this because Maime lived with us in her last years before she died. In a violent fury Maime took the washstick out of the boiling water where she was washing clothes. A washstick is shaped like an officer's night stick and can inflict severe damage if used aggressively. Screaming violently from her basement apartment, "you son of a bee, you son of a bitchin bastard, I'll kill you," Maime banged with a vengeance on Mrs. Higgins door screaming, "Where's your son. Where's your son?" When Mrs. Higgins opened the door, Jim was climbing down the fire escape running, I would imagine for his life. After that incident, Mr. Higgins never touched or dated my mother again.

Recently, my mother told me when she was a little girl attending Joseph F. Brandt School, she had to make a doll for art class. Betty, which is my mom's name, made a very beautiful doll, and could not wait to show it to her art teacher. When my mother walked proudly up to Mrs. Guyer's desk with her doll, it was cruelly thrown in the basket. She told my mother that she did not make the doll because it was too beautiful. My mother cried for a week but never told Maime. I asked my mother why she didn't tell Nana. My mother replied simply, "If Nana found out, she would have killed her!" My mother continued and said, "She would have gone to school and physically beat her because Maime always spoke the truth when she was well. There was no question that my grandmother carried most of the family burden upon her shoulders especially after my grandfather died.

Maime had two sayings that always stayed with me in my life.

One was "if you can't say anything nice about a person, don't say it at all." My mother tells me that Maime never spoke ill about anyone, but if you were wrong and hurt her family she would come at you with a vengeance. The other saying is the most beautiful of all. Maime said, "Be thankful you can help and not the one that's begin helped." Although Maime only went to the second grade, she possessed a great deal of wisdom because she learned by living. In the great first Lady Eleanor Roosevelt's book, "You Learn By Living" she tells how she overcame the fear of coming down with the flu in 1918 that killed many people in Washington. She said,

> *"When the epidemic reached Washington in 1918, it proved to be a major catastrophe in the overcrowded city. I went there every day and came to know some of the people and to realize when there were curtains drawn around the bed that someone had died or was dying. And I forgot to be afraid myself in my thankfulness that I could, in some small way help them."[3]*

Maime and Eleanor Roosevelt said the same thing: "Be thankful that you can help and not the one that's being helped." Both women were ordinary and extraordinary people.

When my Uncle Rudy Pflug came home from World War II in Europe, he married Ann Cacharta. On a hot summer day in 1949 the entire family went on a picnic to Cold Spring Lake. I was four years old and have never forgotten that day. My uncle went into the water with his wife and within seconds he was swept away by an undertoe in the lake. He had fought in Germany and by a freak accident at the young age of 25, Uncle Rudy, Maime's youngest son, had drowned. My aunts were crying and screaming as my uncles brought them up from the lake. After this terrible day, Maime lost most of her strength and vitality for living. In 1966, Mary (Gil) Pflug was laid to rest. She was a woman of courage that defended her family and worked at any job to make an honest living. Nothing was ever below her as long as it was honest. She was a wonderful woman of courage.

Natalie (Dolly) Garvante married Anthony (Marty) Sinatra on February 14, 1914 at City Hall in Jersey City and moved into a four story eight family building on 415 Monroe Street in Hoboken. Dolly, Cookie and Maime walked the same streets in Hoboken but lived in different areas of town. The Shiraks lived in Willow Terrace, which I describe as the demilitarized zone or DMZ since the Terrace separated the Italians from the Irish and German population at the time. The Pflug family would buy their house in 1918 at 814 Bloomfield Street, and 17 years later the Sinatras would be moving around the corner at 841 Garden Street.

Dolly Sinatra was a charming, good looking woman, mainly responsible for breaking the ethnic caste system that existed in Hoboken in the 1920's and 30's. She spoke many dialects as did my grandmother Cookie, and was able to converse at any level, whether it be with a longshoreman or a sophisticated, fast talking politician. She became a very powerful political force in Hoboken and was a woman ahead of her time. Dolly built an organization her way by helping Italian immigrants, as well as anyone whom she thought was in genuine need of help. She had a passion for living along with a burning desire to get ahead for herself and most importantly her family. Since I did not know Dolly personally as I did my two grandmothers, I can only describe what the people who knew her thought when she lived in Hoboken.

My Aunt Helen (Shirak) Romano knew Dolly. My aunt is very religious, constantly praying and writing letters to the Pope at the Vatican. I asked her to tell me about Dolly and she replied, "Dolly was good. She was real good." When someone in Hoboken tells you "you did good or that you are good," you have ultimately received the highest compliment. She then continued, "Uncle Charlie and I used to go to his father's house at 700 Clinton Street, and Dolly used to come over on Saturday to visit Uncle Charlie's sister, Rosie Romano. Dolly was always smiling and full of life. Uncle Charlie used to play the piano and Dolly used to sing and make everybody happy. I used to sit in the corner because I was very shy. Uncle Charlie used to call me Coboosh meaning "cabbage head" in Polish because I never said anything. Dolly and Uncle Charlie sang together 'A Shanty in Old Shanty Town.' This was one of Dolly's favorites. They also loved to sing 'When my Baby Smiles at Me,' by Ted Lewis. All I could add is that we all liked Dolly, and these were the good times. She and Uncle Charlie used to have a lot of fun singing together. She did a lot to help people and did a lot for the churches. Dolly was good."

When I spoke to Tony Calabrese, who bartends at Romano's Portofino's at 700 Clinton Street in Hoboken, he recollected the following: "When I bartended at Romano's down on Jackson Street, Dolly and Marty Sinatra would come in on Friday evening. We would play Frank Sinatra songs on the juke box and Marty would sit there smiling. He would then stop and ask anyone who was at the bar, "Is he that good? He's not that good is he?" You knew deep down that Marty was extremely proud of his son, but Marty was not a man to brag. He just sat and had a few beers and listened to his son sing.

Dolly was busy raising money for all sorts of charities. She was extremely dedicated to St. Joseph's home for the blind and St. Joseph's Church. Whenever Dolly wrote to Frank for a contribution, he would respond by sending her money. I can only tell what I observed as a bartender and what I witnessed while tending bar. Dolly had a good heart and both parents were extremely proud of their son." As the author of this book, I can only add that the sisters of St. Joe's still come to our store, Lepore's Chocolates, every holiday. St. Joe's is still a very poor church and just recently had to close the elementary school. I could see why Dolly Sinatra had so much love for this little church, because the people affiliated with St. Joe's always had tremendous compassion for the poor. This interview with Tony Calabrese took place at the same building where Dolly and my Uncle Charlie sang and danced to make people happy over 55 years ago.

Cookie, Dolly and Maime were just the same. I will now tell you about the other side of Dolly. The incident happened at the plush Westmont Country Club in Bergen County. The gentleman who told me this amusing anecdote wishes to remain anonymous but was an actual eye witness to the happening. Jerry Molloy, who was a very famous toastmaster in Hoboken, was very close to the Sinatras and invited them to a wedding at the Westmont County Club. During the banquet, an announcement was made that Frank Sinatra was performing in New York but might be coming to perform at the Westmont Country Club. After the announcement, one gentlemen stood up and said very sarcastically, "Yea, the only way he'll come here is if he gets paid for it." Dolly was sitting across the way with her husband Marty. Without any hesitation, Dolly bolted from her seat running across the room and really clocked the antagonizer. The eye witness went on to say "I mean she really clocked him." In our town, clocked means that you just got hit with a crushing blow to the head. The fight was on Hoboken style. Marty immediately rose up and said: "Oh Dolly, come on," but she continued her assault. Finally, the fight was broken up and as Ted Lewis would say, "Is everybody happy?" I thought this story had some merit in understanding the personality of Dolly Sinatra. She gave to all sorts of charities and knew her son might be coming to sing in the honor of Mr. Molloy. Because money was never her primary motive in life, it is apparent why she took umbrage at such a caustic remark.

Dolly, Cookie and Maime possessed very similar personalities. They lived with passion throughout their lives and were extremely dedicated to their families. They all possessed courage and spoke with conviction. In "Profiles In Courage," written by President John Fitzgerald Kennedy, he states that, "all of us one time or another will stand in the arena to be tested for courage." I feel these extraordinary ladies stood in the arena to be tested many times during their lives. In the closing page of "Profiles In Courage," President Kennedy stated, "The courage of life is often a less dramatic spectacle than the courage of a final moment, but it is no less a magnificent mixture of triumph and tragedy."[6] Dolly, Cookie, and Maime experienced both triumph and tragedy in their lives. They spoke the truth, and their words were good. It was "A

Time That Was."

So why does a man search for rainbows far away?
Well, this much I've learned is true

CHAPTER 6

Nobody Gets to Sinatra, Nobody

A fter the unique experience of running for Mayor, this much I learned was true—I was bankrupt. The real estate investment properties depreciated fifty percent below the price I had paid for them, and the Asbury Park home plumeted from a market value of $200,000 to $80,000 in just four years. In three years the $150,000 in cash I worked for throughout my life was gone. To compound the personal economic depression, Mario was stung by a bee, and the overnight stay in the hospital was $5,600 at Jersey Shore Medical Center in Neptune, New Jersey. The greed of the Hospitals and insurance companies is why 40 million Americans do not have health insurance.

Without insurance the treatment for the bee sting would have been $1,200. Since he was insured under the business, he was charged $5,600. The insurance carrier paid $3,000 but the compassionate hospital wanted the remaining $2,600. He offered to pay the $1,000 deductible but the hospital refused demanding the full balance of $2,600. If he did not comply, we would be going to court. We hired a lawyer and paid him $350.00 and an additional $80.00 to have a jury hear our case. When he arrived in court, the judge had already determined the day before that the hospital was in the right. During this time he had not been informed by our lawyer that a judgement had been placed on Mr. Lepore the day before since we expected him in court with us. I don't think he needed a lawyer for this outcome.

The legal system and the hospital hid behind a weasel clause, which at the time was a state law that has since been repealed. The weasel term was DRG or diagnostic related group illness. The Doctor diagnosed Mr. Lepore's bee sting as cellulitis which upped the dollar anti for the hospital categorizing his condition into a more serious illness bracket. Even with cellulitis, the cost would have been $1,200 if he did not have insurance. He is still paying the bill today with a judgement that has tainted his credit, and like 40 million other hard working Americans, without insurance. Why have insurance if you have to pay more money for having insurance?

Mario Lepore

In 1889 the famous economic journalist Clement Juglar wrote, "Paradoxical as it may seem the riches of a nation can be measured by the crime, violence and corruption which they experience."[7] The insightful assessment of his time are the conditions we are experiencing in America, and envy and greed must be curtailed to deter economic Armageddon. The inequitable distribution of wealth is greater today than during The Great Depression with the super rich, who consist of 5% of the population, owning the great majority of the country's assets. The Federal Government uses the inflation myth to raise the prime rate, which punishes what is left of the middle class so Washington can lend 20 billion dollars to Mexico when no Latin loan has been repaid since 1800.[8] Only 30% of Americans have a good credit rating with more poor people in the country today than ever before.

Honest people with good intentions are being stopped by Police for insignificant reasons. The good are being persecuted for easy revenue because it is too costly to trap the real criminals. Everything has come down to money, and there is little of it to go around. Americans live on credit cards just barely being able to pay the interest. We are so buried in debt that we are paying for food we consumed over a month ago. The true fact is that we are paying higher prices because the interest is rolled into the next loaf of bread we purchase. We work longer hours, but the quality of life has diminished. Because there is no money, cities and towns become desperate with many experiencing urban blight. Corruption reigns freely throughout business and government with the help of factitious laws such as DWI and DRG, which translates into $10,000 in fines for a blown headlight and $5,600 for a bee sting. The outcome is personal bankruptcy mental instability and the extinction of the middle class.

After Mario, Frank and me met at I'Medici on July 22, 1992, I took the liberty of writing Tina Sinatra since I had presented her with the Galante negatives when she was in Hoboken filming the TV movie "Sinatra." I sent Tina a copy of a song entitled, "The Last Painted Pony" by Bruce Stephen Foster, the same gentleman who would later co-write Mr. Sinatra's Tribute song, "A Time That Was." We felt the song personified Mr. Sinatra, the eternal child we all are when you are young at heart. On Oct. 8 I received the following letter from her secretary which read:

> *Dear Mr. Shirak:*
> *We are returning the package you sent us since Mr. Sinatra does not accept any unsolicited material. We appreciate your interest in Mr. Sinatra's career. Good luck in your future endeavors.*
> *Lisa Tan*

Just three weeks after Miss Tan's encouraging letter, Dr. Anthony Marsh visited the store. When he told us proudly that he was to be a personal guest of Mr. Frank Sinatra at the Barbara Sinatra's Children's Center, I was in awe and disbelief. My efforts to reach Sinatra had failed with one reward for my attempt at the Hilton—a revoked driver's license. Because Dr. Marsh was a loyal customer for ten years, I was not only happy for him but also a bit envious of his ability to get a personal invitation from Frank Sinatra. He then told us that Mr. John Shields, the Executive Director of the Barbara Sinatra Children's Center, was an old college friend and had invited him to California for the children's Christmas party. Dr. Marsh decided to have two hundred pounds of chocolate sent to the center, and Mario molded a four foot, twenty pound chocolate Santa for the children. Unfortunately, Santa arrived smashed in bits from the plane ride, but nevertheless, we received a gracious thank you letter from Mr. Shields. This unusual occurrence of now supplying the Sinatras with chocolates for their children rekindled my hopes of meeting Mr. Frank Sinatra.

Since Dr. Marsh had seen photos we displayed at the store of Mr. Sinatra, he asked me if I could make him some copies. He thought the pictures would be a topic of conversation when he dined with other honored guests and more importantly with the

Chairman of the Board himself. One week before Dr. Marsh's visit, Jim Reardon and I had completed the first version of "A Time That Was." I had given Jim the concept of Mr. Sinatra's tribute song, and he struggled many hours with the lyrics and the melody. When he gave me his first cut version, I told him I wasn't happy with it. He then told me "that the song was the most difficult project he had ever worked on in his 25 years in the music business." I told him, "I knew it would be since we were attempting something that no one had ever dared to try." We were trying to tell the story of Mr. Sinatra's life in less than four minutes. We then sat down, worked throughout the evening, and finally wrote his song. Although I wasn't satisfied with the first version, I decided to give Dr. Marsh a copy of the song along with the photos he requested when he dined with Frank Sinatra.

When Dr. Marsh invited Mario and I to lunch, I gave him the pictures he requested and presented him with a copy of "A Time That Was" along with scripted lyric sheet for Mr. Sinatra. He agreed to take the song and listen to it but told me he couldn't promise that he would present it to Mr. Sinatra. I understood his reluctance but was willing to try anything, since I believed Frank would enjoy the tribute even if it was, in my judgment, only half finished. I could already envision Dr. Marsh having dinner with Mr. Sinatra. In his suit vest pocket he carried old photos of Mr. Sinatra along with his musical tribute. Would he seize the right moment and give the song to Frank Sinatra?

When Dr. Marsh returned, he came to the store and proudly showed us a beautiful picture of him and his wife, along with Frank and Barbara, which was taken at the dinner party at the Sinatra's estate in California. When I asked about the song, he told me he was unable to make the attempt. Jim had proudly written the following note on the cassette tape hoping Frank would receive his gift:

Mr. Sinatra, Thanks so much for your inspiration. Hope you enjoy this gift we wrote for you! God Bless, Jimmy Reardon

Although Frank Sinatra never received the song, Mr. Reardon has honored our city with "Baseball Was Born in This Town" and "A Time That Was." He can feel he has lived for some purpose.

In September of 1992 I ascertained legal custody guardianship over a 14 year old boy named Baltazar Gonzalez. The Babe Ruth League always enables business to help teenage boys between the ages of 14 and 15 years old and it's a way of giving them back some of the wonderful times I had when I was growing up in Hoboken. This is a very difficult time in a young adult's life as many of these kids have no family and some have been cruelly abused as children. It seemed ironic how we established contact with the Barbara Sinatra Children's Center in California, since we were performing very similar roles in Hoboken.

Susan Gonzalez, Ba's mom, was unable to handle the financial burden she was under and asked me to work with her son as she was fearful that he might get involved with drugs. Mrs Gonzalez had also suffered a nervous breakdown after she had lost her job as a nurses aid which she held for eight years supporting a family of three on her own. Susan was fired because she told the head of the hospital the truth, that the elderly patients were being poorly treated. Without her job she could no longer support her family but refused to accept any form of welfare. Her noble intention of refusing welfare almost caused her to take her own life since she was now without hope being financially destitute.

Since Baltazar's father abandoned the family when he was two years old, I tried to bridge a gap in what we both had need of—a father son relationship. Susan told me instances of physical abuse that she and Ba had suffered and the boy told of personally experiencing drug raids when he was staying with his father in Wildwood, New Jersey. After we got to know each other, he would tell me many things in strict confidence, and I felt good that I had gained his trust. Since Ba is a very bad asthmatic, he had been left back from school on two occasions. I was told by many people that he was not very bright and very irresponsible. Working with kids for 13 years, I saw none of this. On the contrary, I thought he was one of the brightest boys I had ever worked with. In addition to being extremely bright, he is an outstanding baseball player. John Honey Romano, who was born in Hoboken, caught for the Cleveland Indians and I hope someday I will see Ba catching for the New York Yankees.

When people suggest to a young person that they aren't bright, it will take its toll on an individual. The result is low self esteem, and the young adult will do anything for attention. This usually manifests itself in a self destructive form of behavior. I encouraged Ba to take the high school entry tests for three Catholic schools: Hudson Catholic, Marist and St. Peter's Prep. Baltazar was accepted by all three schools not for his ability as an athlete but on his scholastic aptitude. Baltazar, however, chose Hoboken High School, and within two months asked me to transfer him to a Catholic school. I sent him to St. Mary's High School in Jersey City in a very caring environment for young adults.

We sponsored him in an International Baseball Tournament in Europe, and he was selected as first string catcher. He played for the United States against other teams throughout the world such as France, Spain, Holland and Italy. He received the most valuable player award for the tournament which made me extremely proud. When he returned, I was told by the very same people that called him "not too bright" that the competition in the tournament was "not that great" and that's why he won the MVP. I don't know what role people like this play in life, since young adults at this age need a great deal of credit, especially when they have achieved something that no one else has accomplished. Ba seems to be well adjusted in St. Mary's, and his mom is doing extremely well. She is back working hard as ever with the sick and elderly and once again giving of herself. She is an extraordinary woman of courage.

In May of 94 Mario and I returned to the Sands to make a half hearted attempt to get to Mr. Sinatra. Since we were financially drained from Legal Fees, DWI surcharges amounting to twelve thousand dollars, and a five thousand dollar bee sting, we couldn't afford the price of tickets. With an entertainment budget of twenty dollars, I tried my luck on the dollar slot machines. One lucky pull on the slots would give us the $400.00 to see Mr. Sinatra. Unfortunately, Lady Luck did not smile upon us that evening. I chose a one arm bandit with no mercy, and in less than five minutes the hope of seeing Sinatra was gone.

We decided to wait at the bar outside of the Copa Room in Atlantic City hoping Mr. Sinatra might be coming to eat at I'Medici. I brought the same version of "A Time That Was" that Dr. Marsh was unable to present to Mr. Sinatra when he was invited out to California as a dinner guest at the Sinatra's home. Because we could not afford the tickets for Frank's performance, I decided to become a theater critic for the evening. After the show I listened at the bar to the reviews Mr. Sinatra was receiving by the audience, who had just seen him live on stage. People in their twenties were raving over Mr. Sinatra's performance. I heard one young man exclaiming to his wife, "I'm so glad I saw him. I can't believe it. It's the greatest show I have ever seen. My parents told me how great he was. I can't believe he could have been any better when he was younger." Children of all ages from 20 to 80, were agreeing that Mr. Frank Sinatra had given them extreme pleasure by his performance. Although we couldn't afford to see Frank that evening, I felt I was with him as the kid from Hoboken once again showed he was the greatest entertainer in the world.

In the mid sixties Mr. Sinatra performed a live concert at Madison Garden. Rex Reed, the very well known theater critic, reviewed the main event the next day. He called Mr. Sinatra a "bore" and went on to say that Frank Sinatra "has had it." The review lacked class and was extremely vicious and smacked of character assassination. Critics like Mr. Reed should come down off their pompous thrones and listen to the people for a change. It could give them greater insight into what's going on in the real world. Thirty years later Frank Sinatra continues to do one thing better than any other entertainer in the world—make people happy. The great American humorist, Will Rogers once said, "I never met a man I didn't like." Therefore, Mr. Reed, you're nice guy but as they say in Hoboken: "Why don't ya smartin up a liddle bit or else I'm gonna clock ya. Frankie did good. Frankie did real good."

In one month I would turn forty-nine years old. At this age many people are planning early retirement. I was thinking in terms of how I was going to bounce back from abject poverty. My liabilities outweighed my assets two to none while owing over $100,000. I always thought that foreclosures and bankruptcies were caused by irresponsible people who lived from day to day with no plan of action. When I hit the canvas, however, I learned humility very quickly. I recalled a passage from the book of Genesis verses 8:10: *"Like fish caught up in a net and birds in a snare, so too are men trapped when bad times come quickly."* This profound statement from the Bible gave me emotional strength since I now knew I was caught off guard and had to try again.

In June of '94 I decided to leave for Italy for ten days with Mario and his mother Maria. Giovani Sportelli, Maria's father, had recently passed away at the age of ninety-five. I was hoping my visit to Italy would help regain the personal vitality I once had to be productive in life again. We stayed in Bari with Maria's older sister who was also named Maria. Each day we drove by car seeing many beautiful historic sites. The visit to the Vatican made me sense my mortality seeing the actual site where St. Peter was crucified. The tour of the Crypt under St. Peter's took you back 2,000 years in Christianity. When I saw the tomb of St. Peter, I was thankful to have made the pilgrimage. When we visited Pompeii, I realized what a short time we mortals have on earth. The people of Pompeii vanished in an instant when Mt. Vesuvius erupted in 29 A.D. burying the entire population in molten lava. The City of Naples lies below Mt. Vesuvius, and no one knows when this massive volcano will unleash its fury on the residents once again.

The town of Conversano is an ancient city just outside of Bari, Italy. Maria was born in Bari but moved to Conversano as a young girl. Maria met Mario's dad, A.J., during the war and came by herself aboard ship to America, where she raised five children. Giovani Sportelli, Maria's father, fought both in World War I and in World War II. Maria took Mario and me to the Grotto of Castellano where grandpa used to hide from the German troops in World War II. The Grotto is a massive crater one hundred feet down in the earth. Maria's mother, Tina, used to secretly bring food to grandpa and the rest of the men that were hiding in the Grotto in World War II. Since the German Army felt they were betrayed, they were hunting down Italian soldiers. Luckily, grandpa escaped and lived to the wonderful age of 95, never having any serious illnesses during his life.

Conversano is a beautiful town where many residents live in the ancient castle called Torre dei Lussemburgo. Street violence is nonexistent, and the children are very obedient with strong family values. In Italy alcoholism is extremely rare since the Italians integrate their wine drinking around the family meal. The southern part of Italy or Puglia is one of the oldest regions and is one of the most beautiful. Maria took us to almost every church in Italy since she is a very religious woman. Mario and I drove to Manfredonia, which is about two hours outside of Bari. We visited the ancient town of Vieste, which was a very strategic Roman outpost during the Glory of Rome. We saw the "sorrow stone" where in the 15th Century the elderly and the frail were beheaded while the male residents of the town were sold off into slavery as the Turkish fleet ravaged Italy. Finally, we stayed in a beautiful mountain retreat called Mattinatella with our gracious host and owner Angelo Colleta. We walked from the mountain to the Adriatic sea in only ten minutes through beautiful olive groves. Some of the roots of these olive trees existed when Jesus walked the earth almost two thousand years ago. I never knew that being poor could take you to paradise. Finally, we visited Trani where soldiers left from ships during the first Christian Crusade. The Church of St. Nicholas rises majestically into the heaven almost in the same condition when it was built more than 1500 years ago.

In September of '94 Mario and I were off to Provincetown,

Massachusetts, which was the first landing of Pilgrims on Nov. 11, 1620? The Mayflower sailed around Long Point and docked outside of Provincetown? The Mayflower Compact was signed, which was the first written constitution in the name of freedom in the world. Thirty four male pilgrims signed the document along with seven servants.

The reason why I know Long Point so well is that for 7 years, Mr. Lepore swam one mile and a half across Provincetown Bay, which begins from Long Point, along with over 120 other swimmers. Swim for Life is to raise money for the Aids Support group in Provincetown. Mario and one other gentleman have the proud honor of being the only two swimmers to have swum in all seven events since the inception of the swim. Five years ago I attempted the swim and actually made it! Just last year I tried again but this time I was fished out of the Bay. This swim was for strong swimmers because we were experiencing waves over 3 to 5 feet in height.

For about 15 years we return to see a great performer by the name of Lenny Grandchamp, who has been playing at the Moors Restaurant in Provincetown for twenty years. In the Smuggler's Lounge, Lenny plays the piano and sings all the great songs from the thirty's through the seventy's. He looks like Luciano Pavarotti and has the comic delivery of a Jackie Gleason. People come throughout the country to see Lenny. He is a great song stylist as well as a prolific singer and song writer. In his only album, "Someone Cares," he is described as the St. Francis of the music business since he comes to "rescue friends and strangers" in need. Lenny plays at nursing homes for the elderly and church benefits along with performing for disabled American War veterans. If you see Lenny perform, you will always come back to Provincetown as he gives all of himself to make people happy. Although he doesn't command the high price you pay to see a Broadway Show or a night club act, you will experience quite a show for a mere drink and a tip in the piano man's cup. Lenny, what piece of work. What an extraordinary entertainer!

The First Great Lady, Eleanor Roosevelt said that "happiness is not a goal but a by product." She went on to say that the only way you can derive pleasure is to "give of yourself." When you become too overly wrapped up in your own selfish needs, you begin to lose your ties to life, which is the "beginning of death."[3] After visiting Italy and going back to beautiful Provincetown, I began to regain the personal vitality I once had and to give of myself once again. Great performers help you regain touch with reality, but most of them walk the fine line of insanity themselves. They can do, however, what very few people on the this earth can do—bring you happiness by making you forget just for a short time the demands in life and the cruel realities of the world.

Bruce Stephen Foster wrote a beautiful song, entitled "The Last Painted Pony." Ellen Sander had given Mr. Foster the title and co-wrote the lyrics with him. When Bruce read about the dismantling of the famous Asbury Park Carousel, he was inspired to write the song. The carousel is 100 years old and almost everyone from New Jersey rode on the beautiful Merry Go Round with their parents. Bruce remembers his mom and dad riding with him on the carousel as I did with mine. He also remembers riding with his children who are now in their teens.

The theme depicts immortality though the eternal child we all are, that's of course if you are young at heart. At the Sands in July of 1992 we tried to present the song to Mr. Sinatra only because we felt he will never grow old. Since Mr. Foster was one of the writers of Hoboken's Tribute Song, "A Time That Was," I thought it appropriate to end with his song.

THE LAST PAINTED PONY

I am the last painted pony, still left on this old carousel,
They took all the others this morning, down to the antique
*   store to sell*
Though my paint may be crackled and faded I was once quite
*   a steed in my pride,*

*Will the child you once were, come along with me now and
take the last carousel ride.*

*Lovers that kissed to calliope music, now bring their babies
to me*
A boy who can't walk takes my reins and flies free
Once the Governor himself took a picture with me.
*And the soldiers posed with their sweethearts on the day that
they ended the war,*
*Now I am the lasted painted pony still left on this ramshackle
floor.*

*Ran through the park late this evening, feeling my body break
free,*
Stopped for a cool drink of water down by the old willow tree
*And all of the memories you've left here are alive now forever
somehow,*
*though stirrups may rust and reins turn to dust, dreamers
never break down.*
*I am the last painted pony, though I was once quite a steed in
my pride*
*Will the child you once were, come along with me now and
take the last carousel ride.*

From Here to Eternity doesn't seem so far
When we feel so close to you

CHAPTER 7

Let It Be Written,
Let It Be Sung

After returning from Truro on beautiful Cape Cod Bay, I was ready to return to the corporate rat race. At 49 years old, I was broke financially and had to once again hit the interview trail for a job. My first job interview was with the United States Chamber of Commerce for a sales representative job in Bergen County, New Jersey. In the final interview I was not hired by the District Sales Manager, because I was unable to script to memory his sales pitch. The U.S. Chamber of Commerce is a non profit organization in Washington and derives almost all of its revenue by selling subscriptions to businesses throughout the United States. Most of the members are small businesses. In retrospect if I were hired, I don't believe I would have excelled at the position since the method most applied in making a sale is by literally intimidating small businessmen to subscribe by showing them the salesmen's Federal ID credentials. Its unfortunate that such a bullying technique is used by one of the largest non-profit organizations in the country.

The next job interview was with WCA or World Corporate Associates located in the Crown Building across the street from the plush Trump Towers. On the first interview I was told WCA were business brokers selling businesses and charging a fee for their services. After partaking in two seminars to learn more about their business, I assessed that they really made their money by selling ads to desperate entrepreneurs, who wanted to sell their business. When I researched how many businesses were really sold by business brokers, I learned that only about 5% of the deals were closed. Also, being a corporate headhunter in my previous business, I knew how many people were actually hired through the job search process. To me it was simple mathematics that WCA sold ads not businesses. When I went back for my last interview, I was told that I did not script the sales pitch very well but that they would give me another chance to memorize the script. I did not return for the final lobotomy since I could not sell something I didn't believe in. Also, because I owned a small business, I would not like to spend $1,500 for an ad that would bring little or no results.

The week of November 17th Frank Sinatra would once again be appearing at the Sands Hotel. I would continue to interview for employment, but all job hunting activity would cease the week we were going to Mr. Sinatra's performance at the Copa Room. Let me try again; let me try once more to get to Sinatra. This final effort meant another $1,000 since tickets to see Mr. Sinatra were $200.00 each. When you add in a two night stay at the Sands Hotel, you can see what I mean by a $1,000 effort.

When Jim Reardon left for New Mexico in February of 94, he left the tribute song incomplete. It lacked the professional polish Mr. Sinatra was accustomed to, and some of the lyrics needed changes for a perfect product. Therefore, on October 28, I called Bruce Stephen Foster and told him that I was once again trying to reach Frank Sinatra with the song, "A Time That Was."

Bruce Foster had collaborated with Mr. Reardon on many occasions and was extremely interested in the project. When I went to Mr. Foster's home in late October, I gave him a copy of the song. He told me he wanted to make certain the song would meet the professional level of expectations of Mr. Sinatra and viewed himself as competing with the great Cole Porter, Julie Stein, and Nelson Riddle. He told me the song would have to be perfect for Mr. Sinatra. When he said that, I knew I had come to the right man.

I remembered what Steven Speiser had said to me four years ago when I tried so desperately to get "Baseball Was Born in This Town" into the Hoboken's Baseball Day ceremony. "You don't have letter head, Ed." Therefore, I arranged a meeting with Mayor Anthony Russo, whom I had run against for Mayor back in 93. I told him about the tribute song and that it would be complete in three more days. I gave him a copy of the lyrics and told him that Mario and I were going to the Sands on Nov. 17 to see Mr. Sinatra perform in Atlantic City. I then asked if he would commission the song. He asked me what the objective would be. I told him we wanted to make Mr. Sinatra happy by a tribute in song for all he has done through his music. Also, in this way, we might have a better chance of bringing the Frank Sinatra Museum to Hoboken. I also told the Mayor that I had reserved an additional ticket for him the evening of the Friday the 18th. As luck would have it, Mayor Russo was going to be in Atlantic City Tuesday through Thursday evening for the Mayors' Convention.

He pondered momentarily and told me maybe he could squeeze another day in from his hectic schedule since he had never seen Mr. Sinatra perform. He told me to type a draft letter which he would edit and give me the commission I had asked for. On November 3rd, I went back to his office and the letter was ready. Finally, I had letterhead! The letter read almost verbatim of what I had drafted in his behalf, but then I turned to the second page of the letter. It read, *Unfortunately, I will not be able to attend your performance. However, I hope to have the privilege of meeting you in the near future.* I felt as if I had been clocked by Punch Pflug. How

could I present a tribute song to Mr. Sinatra commissioned by
the Mayor who couldn't attend his performance and hope for a
Frank Sinatra to look favorably on a museum in Hoboken. The
letter read:

> *Dear Mr. Sinatra:*
>
> *Last year, I had the opportunity to meet with your
> daughter, Nancy. At that time I was delighted to hear that
> Hoboken was being considered for the Frank Sinatra Music
> Museum. This consideration delighted all the people of our
> beautiful city. Just to give you some indication of the extent
> to which you are revered here; when entering Hoboken, we
> have proudly placed signs that read "Welcome to Hoboken,
> Birthplace of Baseball and FrankSinatra." However, we
> would like to do so much more in your behalf since you have
> given so much happiness to an entire world. The people of
> Hoboken truly love Frank Sinatra. And it is with great
> pleasure that I write you this letter.*
>
> *I, as Mayor, recently commissioned Mr. Bruce Foster and
> Mr. Jim Reardon, two professional songwriters with strong
> ties to Hoboken, to write Hoboken's tribute song to you. Mr.
> Foster is actually the great grand-nephew of the famous
> Steven Foster, who wrote some of his great music in
> Hoboken. Bruce has also been nominated for a grammy on
> two occasions. Mr. Reardon is an accomplished tribute song
> writer and was invited to Carnegie Hall by Mrs. Harry
> Chapin to honor her husband.*
>
> *Mr. Ed Shirak, Jr., one of the proprietors of Lepore's
> Chocolate which provides chocolate to The Barbara Sinatra
> Children's Center, has professionally produced this song in
> your honor.*
>
> *I sincerely hope that you have the opportunity to hear it.
> It's entitled "A Time That Was." Your wife, Barbara was
> also sent a copy of the recording. In reality, you are a tribute
> to the world.*

Finally, it is unfortunate that I cannot attend your
performance at the Sands Hotel in Atlantic City on Friday,
November 18, with Messrs. Ed Shirak, Jr. and Mario
Lepore. However, I hope to have the opportunity and
privilege of meeting you in the near future.
                              Respectfully yours,
                              Anthony Russo
                              Mayor

When I returned to Lepore's Chocolate, I called the Sands
Hotel and asked them to hold a ticket for the Mayor until Friday
Nov. 10. They were very gracious and assured me they would. I
had another week to convince the Mayor to come to the Sands.
Since the staff at the Sands knew Lepore's through our chocolates,
they placed us on their special guest list. We had front row seats to
see Mr. Sinatra! I wrote the Mayor two letters the following week
and tried desperately to see him but I received no response.

On November 5th, the tribute song was complete and
sounded beautiful. Bruce Stephen Foster had accomplished what
he set out to do. Let it be written, now Let it be sung. On November
15th, I made one last desperate attempt to have the Mayor hear the
song. The Mayor was not available. During this time Mr. Foster
was not totally satisfied with his final version and went back into
the studio and worked for two consecutive nights. Bruce had to
perform the following evening, being a full time musician that
supported a family of five, and on Friday, Nov. 18th, he was off to
California working on his new album.

Mario and I planned to leave for the Sands Thursday afternoon
with a magnificent presentation in chocolate for the Sinatras. The
total tribute was close to $20,000 since the song was initially
written back in 1992, which meant additional studio time and
money. The presentation in chocolate was a work of art. Mr.
Lepore molds in chocolate as Michaelangelo created in marble. In
the photo section of "Our Way," you can see the picture of his
final creation.

During Wednesday evening, we tried to determine how to get the song and lyrics to Mr. Sinatra, since nobody gets to Sinatra as you know by now. When Mario was molding the chocolate champagne bottle, it accidentally fell to the floor and split in half. He began laughing and then replied, "You know what, let's hide the lyric sheet inside the broken champagne bottle and when Frank lifts the top off, the sheet music will slide out." It was genius. I then placed a small walkman tape recorder inside a candy book that we sell at the store. The book we chose for Mr. Sinatra was Charles Dickens "A Tale of Two Cities," because of his birth in Hoboken and his journey to California to become the greatest star in the world. For Barbara Sinatra we chose "Oliver Twist" by Charles Dickens because of the wonderful work she does for abused children at Eisenhower. I also enclosed in her gift book a picture of our kids from the Hoboken Babe Ruth League which said "From our kids to yours," along with a picture of the same ballfield Mr. Sinatra played on when he was a boy.

Mario re-created the logo of the Barbara Sinatra Children Center in chocolate. He molded a huge disc in chocolate adorned with five white stars with white ribbon running through the logo saying Barbara Sinatras Children Center. It was magnificent! Mario created his work of art on Wednesday evening so we would be ready to leave for the Sands Thursday at three in the afternoon. When we called Bruce Foster, we were informed by his wife Chris that the song was still not ready. We then spoke to Bruce, and he told us that he would have the finished version at four in the afternoon. Because the chocolate presentation was so delicate, Mario had to disassemble his creation and re-create it in Asbury Park. Mr. Foster arrived at my home at exactly four in the afternoon, while Mario was putting the finishing touches on his Michaelangelo creation. Bruce was pressed for time as he had to perform at McCloons Rum Runner in the evening and was then off to California recording his new album. He left the tribute song with us and smiled as he left exclaiming "Good hunting."

I couldn't wait to play the finished version of "A Time That

THE CREATION MADE BY MARIO LEPORE
(Photo by Dave Marsh)

"From Here To Eternity" doesn't seem so far, when we feel so close to you"

Mario Lepore's creation in chocolate of the logo of the Barbara Sinatra's Children Center and a magnificent champagne bottle for Mr. Sinatra along with the lyrics of "A Time That Was." The two books below the chocolate creation are from Charles Dicken's "Oliver Twist" and "A Tale of Two Cities." "Oliver Twist" represents the work Mrs. Sinatra has done for abused children and "A Tale of Two Cities" symbolizes Mr. Sinatra's rise to stardom from Hoboken to California to become the greatest star in the world.

Was." When I heard the song, I tried desperately to like the new version, but something was wrong. It seemed the song had lost the emotional impact and the melodic balance it initially had. I played it again and something very strange began to happen. The song became full of distortions ranging from breaks in the orchestral arrangement to electronic disturbances in the tape. It seemed as if some outside force was telling me to go with the first version of the song. I had three newly produced tapes from Mr. Foster and I played them all. The same distortions occurred on the other two tapes as well. After all the hours that he had put into the perfect arrangement, I selected Bruce's first rendition. We then hid the small juke box inside the book entitled "A Tale of Two Cities" and Mr Lepore sealed the magnificent presentation. At last, on to the Sands!

We arrived at the Sands Hotel in Atlantic City at six in the evening and promptly went to our room to make certain the presentation would not be damaged. I called the front desk and asked for Dorothy Uhleman. The clerk told me no one by that name was staying at the Sands. I then told them that we had a presentation in the honor of Mr. Sinatra, and I was informed that the Sands could not accept or divulge any information regarding the Sinatra's. We knew Dorothy from our past dealings, and I was certain that I would see her before Mr. Sinatra's performance Friday evening. Mario and I decided to eat at I'Medici Restaurant that evening hoping we would get lucky, meaning we might come face to face with Francis Albert Sinatra once again.

At 9:30 in the evening we arrived at the restaurant and were escorted to our table by the Maitre de, Dante Brunelli. He remembered Mario and me from the night Mr. Sinatra spoke to us. After we had ordered our meals, Mario looked up at the dais and discretely told me that Frank Sinatra Jr. was dining with the members of his orchestra. We assumed that they were part of the band because they were talking about musical arrangements as well as singers and songwriters. I called the waiter and asked him how I might be able to speak to Mr. Sinatra. He also remembered us since he was present the evening we met with Mr. Sinatra. Dante Brunelli came over to our table, and I showed him a copy of the Mayor's letter as well as the tribute song that we wished to give to Mr. Sinatra. He advised me that the best time to talk to Frank Jr was when he and his guests were ready to leave. When Mr. Sinatra paid the check for the evening and rose to leave the restaurant, Dante told him of our intentions. Mr. Brunelli made certain that our mission was noteworthy since he scrutinized the Mayor's letter before he spoke to Mr. Sinatra. Remember, letterhead? Mr. Sinatra came over to our table, and I rose to greet him. I told him of our tribute to his dad, and I felt he was genuinely impressed by our mission. He replied, "That's very kind of you. That's very nice. We should talk." When I tried to present him with a copy of the lyrics to the song he refused, and said firmly, "I can't accept that, you have to go through proper channels." He asked me if I knew Dorothy Uhleman and I said "Sure, we know Dorothy." He then told us that the Sinatras would not be arriving till Friday, which hurt our plan of getting the presentation to Mr. Sinatra because we were now under a time crunch. I then learned that the Sinatras were scheduled to make a benefit stop in New York Friday afternoon and would not arrive until later in the evening.

Mr. Sinatra had just performed 3 days in Ledyard, Connecticut and was off in the morning to New York City and then on to the Sands to perform three nights consecutively. I would say that's a tremendous amount of personal vitality at the age of 79. I thanked Frank Jr. for his time, and we were off to the Casino to lose some money. Before we did that, however, I offered Dante Brunelli a tip for introducing us to Frank Jr. He graciously refused since he knew our efforts were genuine. The next evening I gave him a picture of Mr. Sinatra from my Uncle Jimmy Galante's collection. It's one you can see in the book of Mr. Sinatra standing outside of my grandfather, Punch Pflug's plumbing store, at 105 Adams Street, 70 years ago.

When we woke Thursday morning, we drew the curtain from our hotel window to see if the forecast was as ominous as the weatherman had predicted. To our dismay it was raining very heavily with high gusts of wind. All we needed now was a Noreaster. Fortunately, the storm dissipated and by four in the afternoon, the rain stopped. Because of the inclement weather, I had worried that the show might be cancelled, but now I knew we would see Mr. Frank Sinatra.

Mario and I decided to bring the tribute presentation up to the 19th floor of the Sands at six o'clock in the evening. We received word that the Sinatra party was running late because of the weather, and the lengthy benefit Mr. Sinatra had attended in New York. We stepped on the elevator from the tenth floor with Hoboken's magnificent tribute and reached our destination—the executive towers on the 19th floor. As we walked to the front desk, people began marveling at Mr. Lepore's creation. How beautiful, they exclaimed, "Oh! Mr. Sinatra is going to love it!" An older gentlemen and his wife were highly complimentary. He then introduced himself to me as Mr. Singer. I couldn't believe that it was the same Mr. Singer who owned the largest Supermarket in Hoboken. Originally, the supermarket was the site of the beautiful Fabian Theater. As a young boy, Mr. Sinatra used to go to the movies frequently where he would treat his friends with the extra money his mother Dolly used to give him. I, as a young man, used to frequent this splendid theater as well. The Singers were very gracious and wished us the best of luck trying to see Mr. Sinatra. I also noticed many familiar faces going into the executive plaza club. Although I didn't know these people personally, I began to see that many of the groups were from Hoboken. I believe that this would have made Mr. Sinatra very happy seeing many people from his home town coming out in his honor.

The concierge told us that Dorothy Uhleman had not arrived yet but that he would give her our presentation as soon as she arrived at the hotel. As luck would have it, the doors opened from an elevator right next to me and Mr. Lepore, and guess who was standing in the wings? Dorothy! She looked as if she had a very tiring day in New York. She started out from the elevator, and

Mario Lepore and I exclaimed in unison, like two choir boys, "Hi, Dorothy." Since she did not recognize anyone scurrying about on the 19th floor, she seemed to have no choice other than to break out with a great big smile, which reminded me of the Cheshire cat in "Alice of Wonderland." She walked over to the desk, and the inquisition began. "What's that," she exclaimed. "What's this? Who is this for?" I had to say something spontaneously because I saw she was getting irritable. Again, I said the wrong word, Mayor. I remembered the last time I said the magic word, I wound up in handcuffs. I told her: "Dorothy, the Mayor is sorry that he could not be here for the presentation honoring Mr. Sinatra." She stopped me right there. "Mayor, what Mayor? Presentation, what presentation? There's no presentation. Come on you guys! Just come on and get out of here." I then showed her a letter from the Barbara Sinatra Children's Center, and she became thoroughly confused. "Barbara Sinatra?" She exclaimed, "What are you talking about! I thought you told me this was a presentation for Mr. Sinatra." Then she saw the Lepore logo seal on the outside of the seal wrapped creation. "Oh, I've seen this seal before. I know you guys. Oh, now I remember. Weren't you here just last year giving me something?" I told her that we had given her some old Sinatra negatives that she gave to Tina Sinatra. She then saw our personal note attached to the front of Mario's creation which read: *From Here to Eternity Doesn't Seem So Far When We Feel So Close to You.* She asked in a dictatorial manner, "What's this supposed to mean?" I explained that From Here to Eternity is infinity in time. But, we the People of Hoboken feel so close to Mr. Sinatra although he is miles away and are extremely proud of his accomplishments. I wanted to say more about the inner meaning of the lyric but knew Mr. Sinatra would understand if he received Mario's creation.

     She then regained her composure and stated: "Just leave your package over here. I'll make sure he gets it, and they'll be talking about it for weeks." I then gave her a personal envelope for herself. It contained the letter to Barbara Sinatra, a copy of the lyric sheet of "A Time That Was," a personal letter to her, along with a copy of the Mayor's commissioned letter so there would be no misunderstanding. Frank Jr. had told Mario and me at I'Medici that we would have to go through proper channels when we spoke to him less than 24 hours ago. I therefore made certain that I complied with his request to the full letter of the law. I covered all the bases as they say in the business world.

Mario and I then went back to our hotel room to prepare for Mr. Sinatra's performance. After we left Dorothy, I had many concerns when we went back to our room. If Mr. Sinatra receives the tribute, he might be furious that the Mayor was not present. How could this be a genuine tribute if the Mayor is not present? After all, he personally commissioned the song. To protect the Mayor as well as the many hours of exhaustive work and money that went into the project, I sent a letter to the Barbara Sinatra's Children Center one week before the performance requesting an additional ticket for the Mayor explaining that the performance was sold out! I was gambling that this would be the case since from the past experience Mr. Sinatra's performances were always sold out two weeks in advance when we would request tickets from the Sands box office. Most importantly, I couldn't bear seeing Mr. Sinatra opening his tribute along with Barbara, and then getting the closing remarks in the letter:

> *Finally, it is unfortunate that I cannot attend your performance at the Sands Hotel in Atlantic City on Friday, November 18, with Messrs. Ed Shirak, Jr and Mario Lepore. However, I hope to have the opportunity and privilege of meeting you in the near future.*
>
> *Respectfully yours,*
> *Mayor of the City of Hoboken*

I thought it bizarre that Frank Sinatra, an American Hero, the greatest performer in the world who has been with Presidents, Kings and Queens once again would receive a rejection letter from

Hoboken. Obviously, this was not the Mayor's intention. The Mayor's letter was truthful that he was in Atlantic City for three days and had to get back to Hoboken. In my mind, however, I had felt confident that I would be able to convince him to come to the Sands up until the Wednesday we departed for Atlantic City. As I said I was not able to see the Mayor after I received the commissioned letter on November 3rd but tried so desperately for him to hear the song. I felt so certain that his presence would have made a significant difference for our city and most importantly a genuine tribute for Mr. Sinatra. As my luck would have it, the Sands was more than gracious in holding tickets for us up until two days before Mr. Sinatra's performance. I guess you could say that I told a white lie about the performance being sold out to cover the Mayor in the event that Mr. Sinatra received the tribute. In retrospect, I would have done the same thing especially when I tell you what transpired later on in the story. Because the sole purpose of the tribute song was to make Mr. Sinatra genuinely happy, I couldn't see him disappointed just because of a communication breakdown. After all, who would be hurt? Mr. Sinatra and our city once again. The following letter was sent to the Mayor to convince him to attend.

> *Dear Mayor:*
>
> *I earnestly feel your presence at Mr. Sinatra's performance at the Sands on Friday, November 18 would play a very vital role in accomplishing our objective. As I mentioned to you, Mayor, we are on Mr. Sinatra's special guest list for the evening through our business role we play at the Barbara Sinatra's Children's Hospital in Rancho Mirage, California. It would be great if business and municipal government could come together to bring something wonderful to Hoboken, The Sinatra Hoboken Museum. For the life of me, I can't see the Museum going any other place but Hoboken. Pilgrims travel to Jerusalem and Bethlehem to see the birthplace of our Lord. Tourists*

flock to Graceland to see the King, Elvis Presley. People come daily to Central Park in the honor of John Lennon of the Beatles, Strawberry Fields.

Without a doubt, Mr. Sinatra is considered the greatest performer in the world. He has been given the name of Chairman of the Board and the World's Greatest Roman. I feel people would come from all over the world to see a Sinatra Museum where he was born. This is life and vitality—not just a Museum.

I know you run a hectic schedule, but my business instincts tell me the time is right for the Mayor to go to Sinatra on Mr. Sinatra's special guest list. If I were a portentous individual, I would not have lost all my money in real estate. However, I do know that no other Mayor made the attempt to personally express to Mr. Sinatra what he means to Hoboken. Maybe this is what he is waiting for? I don't know. But we don't know unless we try.

As I closed in one of the debate issues we had at Hoboken H.S. I will do so again. Ars Longus. Vita Brevis. Life is short, but Art lives forever.

Sincerely,

Ed Shirak Jr.

After deliberating in our room for about 30 minutes, Mario suggested that I go back up to the 19th floor to make certain the presentation was brought to the Sinatras. At this point I was so emotionally drained, I told him to go and check on the outcome himself. He replied: "Oh no rocketman you started this and now you have to finish it." He began calling me rocketman because of all the letters I had sent in an attempt to meet Mr. Sinatra. Finally, we agreed to go together. When we got off the elevator, I saw Mario was right! The $500 presentation, which took Mr. Lepore five hours to make, was cast aside in an obscure corner with no one concerned of its intention.

Since I have been a Chicago Bear fan for over 35 years, I am used to rejection. However, being half Polish I possess a Mike Ditka temper when things go wrong. I burst into a fit of rage and shouted, "Just give the tribute to Mr. Sinatra back to me. This is a disgrace." The concierge immediately gave me the Hoboken tribute but told me he would call into the banquet room and have someone come out and take our gift into "the room." I had no idea of what room he meant. It could have been a room where the bomb squad would inspect all packages for the Sinatras. The front desk once again received a call from Dorothy demanding more bread. Mario and I began playing tug of war with his splendid creation. I was walking to the elevator in a blind rage shouting: "Come on let it go. I've had it. I'll take it back with me, I've had enough!" Mario kept pulling the other way trying to calm me down, saying, "We've come all this way. Just wait. Just wait." At this moment the butler came forward. He extended his huge arms out and asked us if we still wanted him to bring our gift in to the room. Again, I had no idea of what he meant by "the room." This guy looked like Howie Long of the Los Angeles Raiders. Together, Mario and I placed Mr. Sinatra's tribute in the massive arms of the butler, and he did an end around into "the room" where I hoped Mr. Sinatra was staying.

As I heard many people talking in the distance, I surmised it was the banquet room where Mr. Sinatra and his guests were dining. I thought: "What if the butler brought the tribute into the banquet room? If the Sinatra's opened their gift at the table, it could embarrass them. Also, Frank might think that the presentation was just a cheap trick to get him to listen to a song. There are so many negative things that can occur when you are not in control of a situation. Therefore, as soon as the tribute was out of our hands and into "the room," we had no way of knowing if Mr. Sinatra would ever see or hear the song.

At eight o'clock we were ready for Mr. Sinatra's performance. Mario and I went down to the Copa Room at 9:00 and were shown to our seats, which was center stage front row. After we toasted to our uncertain success, Mr. Dan Dreason, an extremely funny comedian, opened the show. Although Mr Dreason was very entertaining, I couldn't concentrate on the opening act because of the anxiety I was experiencing over the presentation, that was now in "the room." When Dan Dreason introduced the maestro, the crowd roared with electrifying excitement. Mr. Sinatra instantly replied: "I'd better be good tonight." Already, the audience was his. He opened with "I Get a Kick Out of You." In the song he changed a line to "you obviously all adore me." The crowd went wild with approval. Although he would forget some of the lyrics to the song, he made up for it with the warmth and vitality he projects everytime he performs. When he sang, "My Funny Valentine" from Pal Joey I was in complete awe. I had never heard him sing it more beautifully. He never missed a lyric, not a phrase or a note. It was masterful. I started thinking, how can he sometimes forget lyrics or use a teleprompter to remember some of the words when in some songs he's better now than he has ever been. Maybe its one of his mystical tricks again making you think he doesn't have it anymore and then he clocks you Hoboken style. When he finaled with "New York, New York" and "Chicago," the crowd rose to their feet with some shouting: "We love you Frank!" Other people had tears of joy in their eyes shaking their heads and applauding wildly, and I was one of them. He's always been the best and always will be.

Miraculously, sitting at the next table from us was a group of people from St. Ann's Parish in Hoboken including children. They lined up with flowers, presenting them to Mr. Sinatra. He took them tenderly from the children and embraced each one of them. Frank Jr, who was conducting the band was motioning to his Dad to take his last bow and leave the stage. Mr. Sinatra just kept embracing the children and exclaiming with sheer joy how much he loved everyone. I don't know if Mr. Sinatra knew the children were from Hoboken, because everyone was trying to get his attention. If he did know the children were from Hoboken, I wonder if he remembered the day he came to sing in Hoboken on Italian American Day back in 1948. That day, some losers threw rocks, but today the children brought flowers.

Mario and I fought our way through the crowd since we had 10 o'clock reservations for dinner at I'Medici. We were already 30 minutes late and did not want to be canceled out, since we were hoping Mr. Sinatra and his staff might be dining at the I'Medici after his performance. We were hoping he received our tribute and might want to meet the people who were responsible for honoring him. When we reached the restaurant, people were already waiting for him to arrive. There were rumors that he would be coming to dine at I'Medici. It was as if people were waiting for Mark Anthony to appear marching in triumph from an overwhelmingly, successful victory. As we waited, Dante Brunelli, the maitre de told us that he thought he would not be here this night especially after the enervating tour he had just come off from Ledyard, Connecticut.

We decided to skip dinner and have a drink at the bar and think about what might have gone on in "the room" where Hoboken's tribute was delivered. We were also anxious that Barbara Sinatra was not at Mr. Sinatra's performance since we felt that she might have stayed in their suite to see what Mario's creation was about while Mr. Sinatra performed at the Copa Room. We saw Mr. Bill Miller, who has been Mr. Sinatra's accompanist for more than 25 years, sitting across from us at the bar. Dejectedly, I told Mario that I had one more rocket left and that I was going upstairs to our room and bring Mr. Miller a lyric sheet from the song "A Time That Was." I was prepared for the same reaction we received from Frank Sinatra Jr., which was "you have to go through proper channels." At this point, I didn't care.

When I entered my room, I instinctively looked down at the phone located between two double beds in the room. The red message light was on, meaning someone had called. Deep down I was hoping and praying that it was from the Sinatras but at the same time hoping it was not. Did we accomplish our mission making Mr. Sinatra happy, or was it presented in the wrong manner, or was it the Police calling thinking we were trying to poison him? Because I can't see very well without my glasses, I pushed the wrong button to retrieve the first message. It automatically erased one of the first of three messages. I tried again and in my haste I erased the second message. In an instant the operator came on the phone and told me to stop what I was doing. Simultaneously, I heard the voice of Dorothy Uhleman. "Mr. Shirak," she stated in a very genuine and apologetic manner, "I'm sorry for what I said to you this evening. It was a rough day and I want you to know that I am sorry." I stopped her immediately and said, "God bless you Dorothy, I understand." She then told me the following: "The Sinatras got your presentation and it is in their room and we did exactly what you told us to do. Before you leave tomorrow call me." I then asked her what would be a good time to call knowing that Mr. Sinatra is a night person like all entertainers. She then replied tersely, "Goodbye," and hung up. Again I was a little confused from a compassionate apology and then call me tomorrow and "Goodbye." In my letter I had given Barbara Sinatra instructions on how to dismantle the gift to make certain they would hear the song. I now believed I was going to meet Mr. Sinatra and couldn't wait to tell Mario, who was probably starring dejectedly into space, at the bar outside of I'Medici.

When I returned to the bar, Mario asked me about the final rocket. I told him that there would be no more rockets. He then asked about the lyric sheet and why I was not going to give it to Mr. Bill Miller, who was still at the bar. I then said I wanted to have a drink and make a toast. He, of course, wanted to know why. I told him proudly, "we got to Frank Sinatra and that they received the presentation. It's finally over, Mario. We did something no one else could do. We got to Frank Sinatra!" I told him I thought we would meet Mr. Sinatra before we returned to Lepores since Dorothy Uhleman advised me to call her tomorrow before we left the Sands. We then started to joke about the cassette player since I had pasted an orange decal on the play button to make certain Mr. Sinatra would press the right button which would play his tribute song. The button said Push to Play just like a jukebox. I could see

Mr. Sinatra saying to Barbara: "What are they kidding me! Push this? Hey, I'm from Hoboken. Some of those people threw fruit, and some even threw rocks and they want me to push this."

We had hoped that Frank and Barbara would be alone after Mr. Sinatra's performance where they could both enjoy the meaningful lyrics and beautiful melody created by Bruce Foster and Jim Reardon. We could only speculate on what went on in the room that evening. Needless to say, Mario and I celebrated until one o'clock in the morning feeling certain that we would meet Mr. Frank Sinatra. It was impossible for me to sleep that evening thinking about what would take place in my meeting the next day. When we both arose at 8:00 in the morning, I prepared a final letter to Mr. Sinatra telling him what inspired me for almost 3 years in my attempts to reach him. For 2 years I carried a black high gloss folder, which had the picture of the young teenage Sinatra staring across the Hudson looking at Maggio, the character Mr Sinatra portrayed when he won the academy award in "From Here to Eternity." The message I tried to convey was that Frank and Maggio are one and both were from Hoboken. Although Mr. Sinatra achieved ultimate stardom, he started here on the banks of the Hudson, but his legend will live on from here to eternity. I wrote the following:

> Dear Mr & Mrs Sinatra,
> All I ask is that you accept my inspirational portfolio on the total truth on a journey that took 3 years to get to the greatest star in the world to honor him. —Ed Shirak, Jr.

As I was about to call Dorothy, the phone rang. Dorothy beat me to the punch. She wanted to know why I didn't call her. I told her that I was just going to call and come up to the 19th floor. Immediately, she responded, "Come up? What are you coming up for? You don't have to come up." Obviously, I was very confused once again. I told her I had a special gift for Mr. Sinatra, and she fired right back, "Now what?" She reluctantly gave in and told me to come up. I wanted Mario to come, but he told me that this was my day and I should go alone. When I reached the 19th floor, I was told by security to go right into her office. I walked right past Dorothy's room by mistake and finally turned around knowing I had gone too far down the hotel corridor. I saw Dorothy peering out of her office looking for me. I then exclaimed, "Hi Dorothy!" She told me to "keep quiet," that the Sinatras were sleeping. She invited me in and asked, "Where's the other guy?" I told her he was packing and that we had to get back to our business in Hoboken. I then asked her if the Sinatras enjoyed the chocolate presentation and, most of all, the tribute song. She told me she didn't know. All she knew was that Mario's creation was in the room with the Sinatras. This confused me once again since she had told me last evening that the Sinatras received our gift and followed the directions in the letter precisely. Once again, I felt something did not make sense.

I gave her my inspirational black folder of Mr. Sinatra and Maggio and asked if she would give it to Mr.Sinatra. She shook her head as if she would and then asked if I wrote the song. I said yes and gave her another copy of the lyric sheet. When I handed her the folder, a small tootsie roll, dropped out. The Tootsie Roll factory was located in Hoboken for many years before the company moved out in the late 50's. I also knew it was a favorite candy of Mr. Sinatra. When she saw the tootsie roll fall out, she exclaimed, "What's that?" I said in an assuring demeanor, "a tootsie roll. It's just a tootsie roll." "Oh, you guys. You guys are something," she replied. Before I left her I asked, "Can I hug you Dorothy?" She sheepishly responded, "Well, ok." We said our good-byes, and Mario and I were back on the Garden State Parkway heading once again for Hoboken.

We both couldn't believe that with all the work and effort that we still were not certain if Mr. Sinatra had heard his tribute song. We left Atlantic City with a very empty feeling. The tribute presentation was in the "room," so we were told. While Sinatra slept, anything could have happened. Once again, I heard Sid

Mark's comments loud and clear, nobody gets to Sinatra, nobody. On November 22nd I began to write "Our Way" because I was now totally obsessed in getting to the greatest star in the world.

When I began researching and writing simultaneously, I discovered the first forty four pages of Kitty Kelley's book contained negative statements by people that I knew. I found myself writing, researching and interviewing city residents and began to see that many facts were distorted. Of the fifty interviews I conducted, I was able to appreciate the real story about the Sinatra's and their life in Hoboken. I hope you find these stories interesting.

Let us tell you the story, Our Way for you.

CHAPTER 8

In Your Honor, Sir

The famous American poet and author, Carl Sandberg, personified Chicago as "City of broad shoulders and hog butcher for the world."[10] To me Hoboken is a "City of cold shoulders but a city with a big heart." Many people have suffered from a severe inferiority complex by believing what people on the outside derogatorily say about our small town. When I was growing up in Hoboken, I always thought the town was aesthetically beautiful, especially at Christmas time when the city was decorated so tastefully, just as it remains to be today.

When I was hired as a mailboy at the Thomas J. Lipton Co. in Hoboken back in 1961, I worked with many wonderful people who were born in Hoboken. When Lipton moved to Englewood Cliffs, most of the Hoboken people decided not to venture out to unknown parts in Bergen County, which was only 11 miles away. Ironically, the Rustic Cabin, where Mr. Sinatra got his first singing start on his rise to stardom, was located just one block away from Lipton and where Mr. Sinatra first met the famous band leader, Harry James. To this day, many of my friends who have left

Hoboken, will not openly admit that they come from the city because it may damage them socially with the new acquaintances they have made in their lives. Just think, Baseball and Sinatra and being ashamed to admit that you're from Hoboken.

At 24 years of age, I found myself in a fairly responsible position at Lipton, and remain thankful that the company paid my entire tuition for college at night while I worked during the day. After eight years, I left Lipton to join Church & Dwight, Inc., makers of Arm & Hammer Consumer products in New York, as Corporate Employment Manager. When you are doing a good job professionally, people want to get to know you personally and the first question they would ask is: "Where are you from, Ed?" When I said Hoboken, they would reply: "Hoboken, I never met anyone who came from Hoboken." It seemed that the doctors, lawyers, and Harvard School graduates did not want a kid from Hoboken counseling them on whom they should hire. After all Hoboken is blue collar; Hoboken is ethnic. I began to dread answering the question. It seemed when I told them I was from Hoboken my credibility as a professional became questioned. Finally, I decided I needed a weapon to disarm their pompous inquiry as well as change their perception of the historic city. When I was asked, "Where are you from Ed?" I would immediately respond proudly, "I'm from Hoboken, home of Frank Sinatra." Off balance by my remark, they would usually reply, "Sinatra comes from Hasbrook Heights doesn't he?" I would simply respond, "No sir! Mr. Sinatra comes from Hoboken." "Really," was the next stultified remark from my inquirer. I had found the solution that would make me their equal. I was now accepted by my peers as well as my superiors. When I would walk down the corridors at the office, I would now be greeted warmly. The dialogue was now "Good morning Ed, How's Frankie today?" I would say, "Oh, he's just fine. I'm going over his house for dinner tonight." The very same executives would go out of their way to come and tell me that Hoboken has really turned itself around." I would simply respond, "Yes, it has." Because Frank Sinatra was an individual to venture out on his own, he helped break the inferiority complex, strangle hold our city has had as we still might be experiencing "cold shoulders" while always having a "big heart."

When Kitty Kelley came to town in 1984, most of the city believed she was writing a book on Mr. Sinatra which would tell about his life in Hoboken. Anyone who knew Mr. Sinatra or his family were willing to give Miss Kelley practically anything she wanted since we perceived it to be a book in his honor. Because Hoboken is still a family town, we tend to accept at face value what we hear. It may sound very naive, but this is true. Kitty first stopped to see Mike Milo at his record shop, who had his own orchestra many years ago, which Frank had sung with on one or two occasions. Mike Milo, who just recently passed away, told Mrs. Kelley to go to my father and uncles' store, Regent Decorators, because they possessed some rare photographs of Mr. Sinatra. These were my Uncle Jimmy Galante's photos, which were the ones I would later give Tina Sinatra. If my uncle were present at the time, I believe he would have used more discretion when he met Miss Kelley. Kitty Kelley walked into Regent Decorators regally dressed with a frozen smile on her face as if she had a peppermint patty under her breath. Since I was present at the time, I saw how interested she was in the poster board photos my Uncle had of Mr. Sinatra. She asked if she could have them to use in her new book. Although my Uncle Richie denied her request, he allowed her to take snapshots of the pictures, since he felt proud that he was doing a service for Mr. Sinatra.

Unexpectedly, the next day, she visited Lepore's Chocolate in Hoboken. In retrospect, my instincts now tell me that she thought she could acquire additional information about Dolly Sinatra since Dolly had also worked as a candy dipper many years ago in Hoboken for extra money to help support her family. If I had known Miss Kelley's true mission at the time, we would have given her a chocolate truffle to taste that she would still remember to this day. Being the author of "Our Way," I would now like to tell Mr. Sinatra that we thought we were doing something in his honor because we were so proud that finally something special was coming out of Hoboken to honor him. I never knew I would ever get the chance to tell the story about what happened in Hoboken when Kitty Kelley came to town. I hope Mr. Sinatra reads our version because this is to honor him in total truth.

The citizens of Hoboken will now tell their story and what was said to Miss Kelley and how some tried to get retractions from her book. We had no way to reach Mr. Sinatra until now, and hope in some way he can understand what happened when Kitty Kelley came to town almost 10 years ago.

The first individual I spoke to was Joe "Gigi" Lisa at the suggestion of Mr. Frank Totaro, who bartends at Michael's Restaurant in Hoboken. When I went to see Joe at his restaurant, Lisa's on Willow Avenue, I told him of my purpose. Since I was President of the Hoboken Babe Ruth League, Joe candidly told me about the misrepresentation of facts that Kitty Kelley had written about him and about the Sinatra Family. Hoboken is proud of the Babe Ruth League, and Joe is also a coach and sponsor. Most of these kids are from broken homes, and some have also encountered child abuse. The Babe Ruth League keeps the kids off the streets and on the playing field, the same ballfield Mr. Sinatra played on when he was growing up in Hoboken. During the summer we have taken the kids down the Jersey Shore, since many of them have never been out of the city. Although Joe is close to 70, the kids talk to him just like he is one of the guys. He also is very generous to the kids treating them at his restaurant.

My interview with Joe Lisa was conducted at his restaurant, Lisa's, in January of 1995: "When Kitty Kelley came to my restaurant, she told me she was going to write a book on Mr. Frank Sinatra. I was willing to help her because I thought it was going to be a good book. I want to say right now that I never cleaned Dolly Sinatra's house on 841 Garden Street. I also want to say that not every young man got a chance to clean Dolly's house.[11] This was trying to make people feel that Dolly was uppity when she moved up town. I was a delivery boy at Balboa's Restaurant, and Dolly,

Marty, and Frank would come in for pizza. The owner of Balboa's would tell me to play all Sinatra music when the Sinatras arrived. Sometimes Dolly would come in with Marty, and they would sing and dance. These were really good times. Marty Sinatra was such a nice guy. He was so easy going. Nothing ever bothered him. Dolly took a liking to me and asked me if I would like to run errands for her at her home on Garden Street. I took the job and this is all I did—run errands. She was very good to me. If I would come back late from an errand, she would say: "Where were you little son of a bee?" I want to make a point here. In those days people used to use these words in almost an affectionate way. I know it may be hard to believe, but that's the way it was. One day she asked me to come over on a Sunday afternoon because the famous Tommy Dorsey was coming to see Frankie. I told her I would be there, but at 14 years old I was a little frightened and decided not to go. I wish I had accepted her invitation.

I remember when Mr. Sinatra came to sing at St. Ann's Church because it was Italian American Day. Manny Action, who now owns the famous Mateo's Restaurant in California, and I knew there were some creeps in the audience that would try something stupid to embarrass Frankie. We found out that they were going to throw rocks as soon as Frank went on to sing. We thought they would be throwing rocks from the back of the stage. Instead the rocks came from up front. Manny, Spike Costello, and I started tear assing at the losers, and they started running for their lives. The only reason why we couldn't catch the bastards was that it was hard for us to get through the crowds. That was the last time I saw Frank until he came back again in 1952. He was up on a float with his mom and dad and he saw me. He yelled out. "Hey, Joe, How are you?" It made me feel good that he remembered me. I would like to tell Frank now that we have always kept the faith. My sons and my grandsons have been weaned on your music. This is not unique in Hoboken, since all Italian families that remain in our city play your music constantly. I wish some day I could take you around to the bars as you did for me one time. I think you would be proud of how the people still remember you as well as your mom and dad. I would also like to say that I married Angela Totaro, who took the famous picture at the Paramount Theatre. Your daughter, Nancy, used that picture in her book as a tribute to you. Angela has been my wife for close to 50 years and I am a proud father and grandfather just as you. I hope I have set the record straight."

Joe Lisa served in the United States Navy as a Signalman in the South Pacific during the war with Japan. His family received word that his Pt boat #19 was sunk in the South Pacific and that he was lost at sea. He was very fortunate since Pt. #20 had gone in first to do battle and was sunk instead. Joe landed in Guantanamo and was at Iwo Jima. He was known as the Midnight Disc Jockey of the South Pacific. He told me of how he converted the entire South Pacific fleet to Frank Sinatra music because that's all he played being so proud that Frank was from Hoboken. Tokyo Rose got wind that Joe was playing Sinatra music and one evening the American fleet received an announcement that Japan knew who the midnight DJ was. After that, Joe had to stop transmitting Sinatra music to the troops.

I remember as a young man when I used to watch "Victory at Sea" with my Dad. One of the episodes at the time visually showed the Japanese Navy sending a message to the American naval ships saying: "Babe Ruth, Go to Hell." I never knew that Tokyo Rose was saying to Hoboken Joe, "Tell Frank Sinatra to stop singing." I do not wish to make light of all the brave young men on both sides that gave their lives for their country. As we all know, war is a terrible tragedy, and no one ever wins. I just wanted to make a significant point that if a man like Joe Lisa would do all this for Mr. Sinatra, how could Kitty Kelley's interview carry any validity. For 10 years Joe wanted a retraction but had no way to proceed until now.

When I met former Mayor Steve Cappiello on Washington Street in December of 94, I told him about the tribute song that we wrote in Mr. Sinatra's honor. I asked him if he would be interested in telling me about his memories of Dolly Sinatra. I couldn't believe that the Mayor would make such radical comments about Dolly and Marty Sinatra that appeared in the book "His Way." The following day the Mayor came to Lepore's Chocolate ready to tell me about how he viewed Dolly Sinatra. He first asked to hear Mr. Sinatra's tribute song. I still call him Mayor to this day because there are certain people in life that always command respect when they have served in office nobly. Mayor Cappiello always maintained balance and harmony in Hoboken seeing the total picture. When I played the song, he commented that it was rather long since he timed it at four and one half minutes. I agreed with his critique but asked, "How can you write a tribute song for Mr. Sinatra and capture his life in less than four and one half minutes?" We both agreed, and he proceeded to speak. "Dolly Sinatra was a woman ahead of her time. She was a woman of vision. She is ahead of most women today who speak of women's rights but do nothing about it. She was a woman of action. Dolly supported me during the onset of my political career. She played a significant role in much of my campaign, which ultimately elected me Mayor of Hoboken. She could speak with a longshoremen vocabulary if she had to and be eloquent when she had to impress the political hierarchy at the time to make her point. I came from a family of 12 and lived in a tenement house in three rooms with one bathroom. Because the bathroom was always occupied, we always had a pot under the bed if someone had an urgent need to go. We called it the "piscerelle." I'm not embarrassed to say it because that's the way it was. During one of my campaign rallies, Dolly sat beside me and was wearing this beautiful hat. Her hats were just as colorful as Dolly was a person. I called her and whispered in her ear: 'Dolly, that hat you have on looks like a piscerelle.' She instantly took her hat off and screamed, 'you son of a bee and hit me on the head with her hat.' I must point out that this was done in a manner of fun that we used to have in our city when people were still able to laugh at themselves. It is always good to step back and laugh a little.

I must now unequivocally state that when I found out what was written in Kitty Kelley's book, I immediately called her organization and demanded an immediate retraction. They told me not to worry about it but the damage was already done. I never even read the book or bought a copy. I was enraged about the outcome. I can only say that I am the only living Mayor from Hoboken who went many times to see Frank Sinatra perform. I always low keyed it because I would be swamped with requests for tickets. I always paid my own way because I was proud to see someone make it from my generation. Why would I make a statement about Dolly when we were friends? As I said, she played an important role in assisting me in my early campaign to ultimately becoming the Mayor of the City of Hoboken."

When John J Grogan was elected Mayor of Hoboken in 1953, Mr. Jim Bailey served as his personal assistant. He recollects Dolly Sinatra in this manner: "Dolly was a famous mid-wife in Hoboken who brought a lot of children into the world. She was very active in politics and was very outspoken for what she believed. She could speak at any level and talk with high society as well as longshoremen. She was very instrumental in paving the way for six of the last Mayors, who were of Italian descent. She was well liked and well received in the political arena and believed in the democratic process. I now live in Fox Hill Gardens and was good friends with Francis Garrick, Mr Sinatra's Godfather. I gave him a picture of Franks' father Marty, and Frank Garrick said he wanted to send it to Frank Sinatra, since he thought Frank had never seen that picture before. I don't know if he ever sent it to him." At eighty years of age, Jim Bailey still patronizes the local bars in Hoboken. He is held in high regard in our city and is known to speak the truth in all matters. His motto is: "if you have a smile on your face and a song in your heart, you will just do fine in life." He loves to sing and tell jokes and keeps people informed on current affairs and is younger in spirit than many people in their thirty and forties.

Mr. Frank Totaro tends bar at Michael's Pub on Adams Street

in Hoboken. When I told Frankie of my idea of Sinatra's "From Here to Eternity," he convinced me to call Sid Marks, the famous radio broadcaster who airs all of Mr. Sinatra's music throughout the country. He thought it might be a way of me getting to Frank Sinatra. Frank is a guy who encourages people when they have an idea and will always contribute to a conversation instead of being critical. Frank Totaro remembers Mr. Sinatra in this way: "When I was a kid I used to shine shoes to make some extra money. I remember once when I shined Frank Sinatra's shoes in Hoboken. I couldn't believe that he gave me twenty five cents. The shine was only a nickel. It was the biggest tip I had ever gotten when I was a kid. This is before Frankie had made it. I remember when a whole bus load of kids from Hoboken went to see his first film, "Higher and Higher." It was playing in New York. The kids on the bus were so proud that Frank Sinatra, a kid from Hoboken, was a star in the movies. There were a lot of people pulling for him from Hoboken. Unfortunately, the people with the big mouths, the jealous ones, spoil it for the people who really appreciate what he has accomplished. I remember when I used to tend bar at the famous Clam Broth House in Hoboken, and Dolly and Marty used to come in. They would come in at least once a week. Dolly's presence was always felt as soon as she entered the room. She would sing and kid around and make people laugh. Marty would enjoy sitting down and eating and drinking beer. They always seemed to be having a great time, and I really believed they loved Hoboken. This was my observation while tending bar. She was always good to me, and we always got along." If you have a dream or need of encouragement, you can see Mr. Frank Totaro down at Michael's Pub in Hoboken on Adams Street. He doesn't charge you for free advice, at least, up until now. Frankie also told me of how Mr. Sinatra tried to sing at the Continental Hotel and was not successful in convincing the owner that he had talent. I remembered having my experience across the street at Signore's Lounge, which was previously named the Continental Lounge, when I announced my candidacy for Mayor in 1992.

Mr. Jack Lynch tends bar at Moran's Pub on the corner of Fourth and Garden Street. Jack is 69 years of age and stands about 6 feet two inches tall. He plays golf regularly and tends bar in Hoboken on weekends. The Sinatra Family was very close to Mr. Jerry Molloy, who was a very prominent speaker and toastmaster. Mr. Molloy was the gentlemen who invited the Sinatra's to the wedding at the Westmont Country Club, where Dolly clocked a certain longshoreman. Jack was all-state in basketball for St. Mary's High School in Elizabeth, New Jersey, and Jerry Molloy was his basketball coach. Jack told me that he and Jerry Molloy would talk almost every day. He then went on to say: "I still know his number OL9-1085. Since I was a Perry Como fan, we would always kid who was better. Jerry always used to say: "Come on, Frankie is the best and you know it. I had a high regard for Jerry Molloy." When Jerry Molloy became ill, he called me from St. Mary Hospital in Hoboken and said: "Guess who was just here?" He then proudly stated, "Frank Sinatra." "I know this visit meant a lot to Jerry, and he always meant a lot to me." If you want to go one on one in basketball someday youngsters, you can visit Jack Lynch Friday evenings at Morans in Hoboken. He'll buy you a pint and beat you on the basketball court. From the basketball court, you can also see Demarest High School, the school Mr. Sinatra attended.

Of all the individuals I spoke with, Mrs. Helen (Fiore) Monteforte provided the most lucid memoirs of Frank Sinatra and his mother Dolly. Helen lived across the street from the Sinatras on 414 Monroe Street and described herself as a "mother hen" to Frank and her younger brother Pat Fiore. Helen remembers Dolly in the following way: "Dolly was a vivacious, beautiful, blue eyed woman with light skin and strawberry blonde hair. She was a real go getter, who was constantly pushing for her family to get ahead. I'm sorry to use this word, but she was a "hell raiser." She would sing gayly and dance joyously right on the table at the famous Clam Broth House in Hoboken. She loved life and had tremendous charm. Dolly was active in every political organization and did a tremendous amount of public service work for the community without being paid. She could light the fire under anyone when she needed something to be accomplished. I liked Dolly very much. When she made up her mind that something had to get done, it would get done. Marty Sinatra was a beautiful man and very quiet, much like my husband. My mother, Margaret (Sevano) Fiore helped assist Frank's grandmother, Rosa Garavante, in bringing Frank into the world. My mother was my best friend and very well read. Although she came from Italy, she spoke impeccable English just as Dolly did. Dolly and my mother got along very well together. Since Dolly was always so busy, she would ask my mother about what she was reading. That was Dolly, always curious and thirsting for knowledge. Although Dolly read extremely well and spoke eloquently, she never sat still for a minute. I think that's why she related to my mother. They maintained a good balance."

"I was the big sister to Frank and my brother Pat. They were both devils as young boys. I remember when Frank and Pat threw firecrackers down an old iron manhole cover. Frank was smart enough to run, but my brother Pat stood there as the manhole cover exploded in the air. Frank was always welcome at our house, and I always believed he was comfortable at our home, since there was always a show going on at the Fiores. I come from a family of seven, and Frank would eat with us occasionally. Because he was the only child in his family, I sensed he liked the family atmosphere in our house. Dolly was always about town very active in business, politics, and charitable matters. Since his Dad was on the fire department, he would work different hours, and many times no one was home at Frank's house. Dolly would not allow him to stay home alone so he would come to our house with my brother Pat. Frank always dressed impeccably well with excellent taste, and always stood out from the other boys. To me, he always had something special. Once Pat and Frank wanted to dress alike so my mother cut their pants and made them both knickers. They were both nuts, but they were good kids. We had family and values, and I consider myself very lucky for those experiences and feel very proud to have been a big sister or mother hen to my brother Pat and Frank Sinatra. I feel very proud to know Frank Sinatra and would like you to know what a giving and charitable person he is. If you ask Frank for money, he will never give you a nickel. But if you need something, he will give you his heart because he has true compassion, which is a rare quality today. There is a big difference between wanting for one's self and having a true need."

On February 26, 1995 I personally met Helen (Fiore) Monteforte for the first time. Up till now, she told me her story by phone as her husband Tony recently suffered a stroke. In World War II, Tony Monteforte was also a war hero just as my uncle Jimmy Galante. For 51 years he has been permanently confined to a wheelchair, after he was brutally wounded on the battlefield in Europe. Helen has been at his side ever since Tony returned from the war. When I met Helen and Tony for the first time, I was astonished to see how young they appeared since Helen is eighty three and Tony eighty eight.

Although Helen has not ventured far from Hoboken, she possesses tremendous wisdom about life and generates true warmth and compassion. As she began to reminisce, about a time that was, she first told me the story of the sliding pond. "My mother looked out the window, and there was Frank and my brother Pat on this incredibly steep conveyor belt that resembled a giant sliding pond. She was trying to call them for dinner but became frightened that they might slide off and told me to go down stairs and get them. Those two nuts were sliding down an almost two story sliding pond where all sorts of animals would slide into a pit. It probably was, now that I think of it, a loading belt for small livestock and chickens. I screamed at Pat to come down as well as at Frank, and they both came flying down. They were both nuts.

I remembered when I went to see him at the Paramount Theater in the 40's when he first got his start with all the bobby soxers screaming and swooning over him. I was in the third row, and he stared down at me and motioned with his hand pointing to me like he knew I was from Hoboken. I pointed back at him, and he nodded and walked off the stage. I never thought I would get a chance to see him again.

In 1984, I was invited by Francis (Frank) Garrick, Frank's Godfather, and his wife Minnie to see Frank Sinatra perform at Carnegie Hall. Because my husband has been disabled for 51 years, I haven't been to many places, but I have no regrets as I have had a wonderful marriage. On the night of Frank's performance, a beautiful black limo pulled up to the Senior Citizens apartments, which is named Fox Hill Gardens. I never knew Frank Garrick was Frank's Godfather until we started talking at Fox Gardens, and as strange as it sounds, he never knew how close my brother Pat was with Frank until we began to know each other more personally.

When we arrived at Carnegie Hall, we were escorted by these big, beautiful muscular guys in black tuxedos. I walked by Sylvester Stallone, Liza Minnelli, and Peter Allen. There were so many stars there that evening. We were taken down to the front row, and the people around us were told by our escorts that these three seats were reserved for Mr. Sinatra. I didn't know they were for us until our escorts motioned that these were our seats and sat us down as if we were royalty. I felt so embarrassed that here we are three little people from Hoboken among these stars and millionaires. It told me deep down that Frank is proud of his small town. From the Paramount to the Carnegie Hall to see Frank Sinatra, I would have to say this is a once in a life time experience.

We were then brought backstage, which is unheard of, to see Mr. Sinatra. When we walked into his dressing room, he was very nervous and irritated. I stood in the back and let Frank Garrick and Minnie do the talking. It was a stormy night, and I sensed he was uneasy and melancholy. He then looked up like he knew us from yesterday and said, 'After the show I have to get on that damn plane.' Since Dolly had just tragically died in a plane crash, I felt very badly for him at the time. He then shifted his conversation to me and asked: 'Which one of the Fiore girls are you?' I said, 'I'm Helen.' He became more composed and said, 'Ah Yes, Helen.' We left Carnegie Hall that evening feeling like stars, and I felt so wonderful that Frank treated Minnie, Frank Garrick and me with such kindness and gave me a special day I will never forget. Minnie, Frank Garrick and me, just three kids from Hoboken at Carnegie Hall to see Mr. Frank Sinatra.

My brother Pat Fiore recently passed away last April. I am very proud of a beautiful letter he received from Frank Sinatra. My brother wrote Frank and for the life of me, I don't know how he got the letter to Frank Sinatra since nobody gets to Sinatra. The letter was written to my brother in 1974, and I will cherish it as long as I live because this is a letter from a man who remembers his roots in our town and his close friend, my brother Pat."

The letter was read to me by Mrs. Monteforte. It was a compassionately moving letter by a prolific writer. It touched on his deep concern for his close friend Pat and the family he knew so well as a boy. Mr. Sinatra mentioned how "rare loyalty is these days" and expressed sincere interest in how his old friend was doing. In the letter he invited Pat for a drink when Mr. Sinatra was performing in Texas, and Pat made that invitation. It is wonderful to know that the greatest performer in the world still has fond memories of the people who stood by him when he was starting out in Hoboken.

Helen (Fiore) Monteforte went on to say that Dolly invited her entire family and paid for everyone when Frank got his first singing start at the Rustic Cabin in Englewood Cliffs, N.J. "Dolly was always that way. She was very generous but also knew the people present would benefit Frank at his shows at the Rustic Cabin." Dolly was an excellent business woman; she was a go getter; she was very active and helpful in her community; she was vivacious and fun-loving; she was a public servant without the title, which meant not being paid for her efforts. I believe this summation of Natalie (Dolly) Sinatra is true testimony to a woman of character ahead of her time — an American heroine, and of Mr. Frank Sinatra, a kid from Hoboken, who became the greatest star in the world.

During Christmas week of '94, I asked many people from our city if they knew the Sinatras. During the holidays we are privileged to see almost everyone from Hoboken because everyone knows Lepore's. Some of the older folks would say: "Frankie was a rough kid and would always be getting into mischief. However, when Dolly was present, he would be good because Dolly taught respect." I was told one story that Dolly owed one of our customer's aunts money for 5 pounds of potatoes and never paid them back. Another women just commented, "I heard she owed money and sometimes didn't pay her bills." I call these statements the "They Say" people. Let me explain what not paying back really means in Hoboken, if you continue to think somebody owes you money. Before money was used as legal tender, society functioned on the bartering economy. I would give you fruit from my store and you would repair my shoes, if you were a shoemaker. People swapped goods and services instead of using money as the medium of exchange. In Hoboken, especially Little Italy or downtown, people had very little money. They would swap for favors and goods and services.

When the Italians settled in Hoboken, they spoke very little English. Dolly spoke many dialects and became an interpreter in court when the Italian people needed representation to help them legally establish a business. Today all municipalities require a CO (Certificate of Occupancy) license when you open up a business. During her times the city also required business owners to have some form of permit to open a business. The Italian people opened up many specialty shops in Hoboken which ranged from bread, pastries, fruit, and salumerias (Italian deli). Quality specialty shops remain a major part of Hoboken's culture today. Dolly Sinatra assisted her people in acquiring the necessary permission to open their business providing a valuable service. In the Barese dialect, the word is called "dimentiche." In the Sicilian dialect, it is very similar. It simply means this is a favor and forget about the money. If you go beyond the story of the potatoes, it is probable that Dolly Sinatra played a major role in helping the gentlemen establish his fruit store. People in Hoboken today continue this practice of "dimentiche." It is known in Hoboken that Dolly Sinatra helped the poor, gave to charities, and got jobs for teenagers doing battle with City Hall. Maybe in "her way" she thought she should be entitled to five pounds of potatoes or other favors she received for the services she rendered helping her people. It appears she was always testing people to see if they valued what she had done for them as a public servant. Although she didn't have the political title of Councilman-at-large, she performed as a "public servant" without pay.

When you study the life of Jesus, you learn that he was brought before Herod the Great and the powerful body of Jewish priests called the Sanhedrin. He was tried by the Roman procurator, Pontius Pilate, for claiming to be the Son of God, saying he would destroy the Temple and for having stirred up the people against Caesar. Jesus was charged with blasphemy and sedition. In the Holy Bible St. Mark says: *"Many bare false witness against him" (14:56)*. St. Matthew says: *"Many false witnesses came" (26:60)*. In the Ten Commandments, of Moses, God said: *"Thou salt not bear false witness against thy neighbor."*[12] During Jesus' life there was deep hatred for him by Rome and Judea as well as fear and jealousy for a man who claimed to be the Messiah. In the Mishna, the basis of the Talmud or traditional Jewish Law, there are three classes of testimony recognized by the law in a trial for life, which are: a vain testimony, a standing testimony and an adequate testimony.[13] A vain testimony was superficial or worthless and could never hold up to convict the accused. A standing testimony obviously carried more weight but had to be later on confirmed with more substantive proof. An adequate testimony was when witnesses agree together beyond a reasonable doubt about the accused just as our court system is structured today. It is perfectly clear that by Jewish Law they had no ground to convict Jesus and therefore brought him to Pilate. Pontius Pilate "washed his hands" and let the people of Judea decide.

"Our Way" rests on sound, living testimony from true

witnesses that devalue what was said in "His Way" by Kitty Kelley. "Our Way" uses not only factual knowledge but common sense and wisdom to explain the culture of our town. Wrongly interpreted facts have a devastating impact on all parties concerned and in this case, it was felt by the Sinatras and Hoboken. The interviews conducted by Miss Kelley were not even vain but inane forms of testimony.

Every Christmas for thirteen years the CBS mid-wives, Carol, Barbara and Sally, have journeyed from New York to Lepores. These three young ladies buy over 50 pounds of chocolate each year for the new mothers they assist bringing children into the world. When a young girl in Dolly's time would become pregnant and was not married, she would be disowned by the family. Disowning a family member was the closest thing to death, especially when one could not speak English. During this time the population of Hoboken was over 70,000 and doctors and midwives would jointly deliver newborn babies. There was no question that Dolly was a famous midwife and brought many babies into the world.

In the book, "Crossing the Threshold of Hope," written by Pope John Paul II, he tries to explain his views on "pro choice." The Chapter is entitled "The Defense of Every Life:" His Holiness firmly rejects "pro choice" but further states that "the woman pays the highest price, not only in motherhood but for the destruction and suppression of the child conceived."[2] From my reading of the book, I felt it was one of the most difficult questions put before the Holy Father, especially with the epidemic of teenage pregnancy affecting the world today. He concludes by saying: "Its better to say no more about this painful subject."

In the Holy Bible, St. John tells the story of "The Enmity of the Pharisees." Pharisee is a word that describes the ancient Jews who observed the religious laws and traditions to the letter. It also had meanings in the Bible as a hypocrite or self-righteous person and has sometimes refers to lawyers as Jesus said according to St. Luke 12: "*Woe, unto you lawyers! Ye have taken away the key of knowledge.*" The word enmity is defined as a deep seeded hate of a man compounded with jealously and fear. Jesus went to the Mount of Olives to pray and later on went to the temple to teach the people. The scribes and Pharisees brought him a woman who they said committed adultery. Since they knew the law of Moses was stoning to death, they tempted him by asking what they should do since they wanted to hear death from the mouth of Jesus whom they hated. Jesus stooped down and wrote on the ground, "as though he heard them not." They continued to ask so they might accuse him in their hate and jealousy of him. He arose and said: *"He of you who is without sin, let him first cast a stone at her."* They were convicted by their own conscience and left the temple one by one and "no man had condemned her."

The following individuals are a few Outstanding Women associated with Hoboken from George Moller's "The Hoboken of Yesterday:" Dr. Sofie Herzog who settled in Hoboken in 1885 had her first residence at 530 Garden Street. She developed a large medical practice and was highly regarded by the town's citizens. She was a familiar figure as she drove around town in her Owens Magnetic, a car controlled by push buttons mounted on the dashboard.[5]

Elizabeth Almira Allen was instrumental in the first state wide teachers retirement law of the U.S. effective in March of 1896. Years later she was instrumental in establishing teachers security with The Tenure Office Act. She was a member of the Daughters of the American Revolution.[5]

Nina Hatfield was the wife of Hoboken's Librarian Thomas Hatfield. Nina became librarian in 1924 after the death of her husband. Mrs. Hatfield became nationally known for her ceramics. In this field Nina Hatfield was internationally famous winning prizes for exhibits in the Paris Exposition.[5]

Mrs. Otto H. Wittpenn/Caroline Bayard Stevens married Otto H Wittpenn before moving back to Stevens Castle. Her work to redeem juvenile delinquents as well as fighting for prison improvements gave her national recognition by President Herbert

Hoover. Her funeral service at the Holy Innocents Church was attended by over 2,000 mourners and President Hoover sent a message of condolence to her family. She was buried in Hoboken Cemetery.[5]

Sadie Leinkauf is the only woman in Hoboken's history to have had a public building dedicated to her memory. Miss Leinkauf's services to the city in the field of education was outstanding. For thirty years, through the administration of A.J. Demarest, Joseph F. Brandt and Daniel S. Kealy, she was a stable force in the office of the Superintendent. She was also one of the founders of the Hoboken Girl Scouts and served for 13 years as Scout Master, Commissioner.[5]

Hetty Green, the richest woman in America, did not contribute to the cultural aspects of the city. She was just rich, real rich! Hetty was born on Nov. 21, 1835 in the famous whaling town of New Bedford, Mass. She gained knowledge of business from her father and later Hetty would shock Wall Street with her astute knowledge in financial affairs. The most important thing in life to her was to make money in any way and then hold on to it for life. She was obsessed with making money and saving it for the sake of having it. She was dubbed by the financial world, "The Witch of Wall Street." It was a time that was when the richest woman in America lived in the uptown section of Hoboken in a cold water flat for $19.00 per month.[5]

Natalie (Dolly) Sinatra was born in Genoa, Italy, and came to Hoboken with her family as a young girl in 1902. Dolly was a beautifully charming woman who married Anthony (Marty) Sinatra on St. Valentine's Day, February 14, 1914. They moved into their first home on 415 Monroe Street and on December 12, 1915, Francis Albert Sinatra was born. During this time the Sinatras were poor like all Italian families who lived in downtown Hoboken. With just an elementary school education, Dolly possessed both intellectual acumen and curiosity along with a burning desire to advance herself in life. She was well read and spoke many dialects helping many Italian people with legal matters, especially those who spoke very little English. Dolly and her husband purchased a bar in Hoboken and called it "Marty O'Briens." She became the first female to tend bar. She would occasionally use the name Dolly O'Brien when she had to make an impact on the political hierarchy to enable her to venture out of the confines of downtown, Little Italy. She was obsessed with changing things for the better of her family and people in the Italian community as she stood firmly against all forms of prejudice. Natalie Sinatra helped the poor and gave generously to charities throughout her life. She built her own political organization and used her newly acquired clout to get jobs for teenagers demanding it of City Hall. She danced gayly on the table tops of Hoboken and sang and laughed about life making people very happy. She was a culinary artist in the kitchen, and it was well known that nobody could cook like Dolly.

She became the most influential woman in the city because she dared to step beyond her boundaries and paved the way for the first Italian mayor, Carmine De Sapio. Although she never held public office, she was a woman of vision who took action fighting for the rights of all people. Dolly Sinatra had a tremendous passion for giving and living and brought many children into the world as a famous midwife. Dolly moved uptown to 703 Park Avenue with her family and shortly after purchased a home on 841 Garden Street and became a woman of prominence. She "looked fear in the face" as she stepped beyond the boundaries of Little Italy remaining faithful to her husband Marty throughout her life. She was a courageous woman who believed deeply in her son, which enabled Frank Sinatra to step beyond the boundaries of a city and then a country to become the greatest star in the world.

Dolly was good. Dolly was real good. She was an outstanding woman from Hoboken and an American hero because she stepped beyond her boundaries and dared to make a difference in her lifetime. Although both my grandmothers were not as visible and influential at the time, I see so many similarities in these extraordinary people. Dolly, Cookie and Maime were just the same.

They were women of courage who spoke the truth. Their words were good. It was "A Time That Was."

The Road may lead back home again—but till it does
There once was a time that was

CHAPTER 9

Reprise

And after all these years, through the triumph and the tears, there's still a smile in those ol' eyes of blue. He's the same man but the journey's brand new. Let him tell you his story, let him sing once again for you. When we wrote the lyrics to "A Time That Was," I thought deeply about what lay ahead for Mr. Sinatra regarding his new journey. I can best sum it up with an excerpt from the letter I had personally written to Barbara Sinatra when Mario and I journeyed to the Sands in Atlantic City to present him with Hoboken's tribute song. The passage of the letter read:

Hoboken's tribute song is entitled, "A Time That Was." Its theme focuses on how a man's dream can become a reality if you bear in mind that "your own resolution to succeed is more important than any one thing." Abraham Lincoln said that since I am not that eloquent. It then traces Mr. Sinatra's early days in Hoboken to stardom up till present where he's still the same man but the journey's brand new. The journey is to be an inspiration to the world through song

and determination to do one thing—make people happy,
which is the essence of life.

When Mr. Sinatra steps onto the stage to perform, he continues his journey giving people genuine pleasure through his dedication to hard work from his "God given talent."

In 1960 Mr. Sinatra founded his own record company and named it "Reprise" (to play again). However, when I researched the deeper meaning of the word, I found reprise had many dimensions relating directly to Mr. Sinatra's life. Reprise is defined as follows: to take again. to recompensate; to pay. 2. a taking away by way of retaliation. 3. a ship or other property recaptured from a pirate or a foe. 4. in music, repetition: now usually restricted to the repetition of or return to the first subject, or theme, of a sonata movement, after the development; recapitulation. When I closely examined an old 45 recording of Mr. Sinatra on the Reprise label, I was amazed to see the picture logo was an old steamboat. In 1804 Col. Stevens, founder of the modern city of Hoboken, erected the first wharves on the riverfront and designed the first screw propeller steamboat. In 1811 the first steam ferryboat of Col. Stevens made its appearance. The Hoboken Steamboat Ferry Company was incorporated 12 years later.[4]

Reprise and the steamboat are related closely to Mr. Sinatra. Beginning his career in Hoboken, he used to ride the Hoboken Ferry back and forth to New York attempting to sing in any club that had a live band; and one in particular, was the Village Inn. Ironically, almost 15 years ago, I first saw Bruce Foster and Jim Reardon perform in a bar also by the name of the Village Inn. Day after day Mr. Sinatra would return by ferry to Hoboken—a form of reprise. When he founded his own company Reprise Records in 1960, it was his way of retaking his own goods taken from him or detained from him by record companies that made a huge profit from his talent. He discovered through hard work how much more he could be recompensated with his own company. With the reprise steamship logo, he symbolically recaptured from his foes what he felt was his. Hopefully, he will now return someday to our city and in musical terms—return to the first subject or theme after the development of his sonata meaning his life. Reprise: to take again, to come back.

After 35 years, in September of 1984, Mr. Sinatra did come back to Hoboken with President Ronald Reagan to campaign on his behalf for the Presidency of the United States. President Reagan was honored with a dinner at St. Ann's Church, the very site where Frank Sinatra sang when rocks were thrown at him on stage. On May 23, 1985, he returned again in triumph to Stevens College to receive an honorary doctorate of engineering during the college's 113th commencement ceremony. As a young man, his father was disappointed with his decision to end his formal education, and Dolly always dreamed of him attending Stevens to become an engineer. Now Mr. Sinatra had fulfilled his parents dreams by returning to Hoboken as a great star and an honorary, degreed engineer. Unfortunately, a third of the 300 undergraduates signed a petition protesting the honorary degree since they felt he had no engineering background. From rocks to jeers in Hoboken— Mr. Sinatra has seen it all.

When he stepped to the podium to accept his degree, he addressed his audience with all the class he has always possessed. "I am honored," he said, "to be a small part of your day." With humility, he addressed the graduating class of '85 as "his fellow students" in his closing remarks, which drew laughter from the audience. In an instant he reverted back to the street fighter he is just as his Dad Marty fought in the ring when Frank was growing up in Hoboken. He continued forecefully, not being shaken by the ignorance of the students and closed with, "I wish you well. I wish you great success in your endeavors. And, I hope that you all live to be 400 years old, and the last voice you hear is mine." This prosphesy will be fulfilled as long as there is music because Mr. Sinatra engineered his own destiny through "hard work" and his "God given talent."

Francis Albert Sinatra is an American Hero and the greatest

star in all the world. I will support this statement our way: Whether it be the star of David having six points or the star of Bethlehem with 5 points, Mr. Sinatra impacts all key points that make him the star of stars. The first point is that he still remains the world's leading performer of popular music, the artist who set the mold for all others to fill. His latest album, "Duets," is already double Platinum, selling over 10 million copies. He has acted in more than fifty films receiving Oscars, Grammys, Emmys and Peabody Awards. There are some people who feel he is a greater actor than a recording artist. His acting ability, therefore, is the second point of the star. The third point is his devotion to humanitarian causes, performing benefit concerts throughout the world and participating in numerous fund-raising drives. The fourth point of the star is that Mr. Sinatra has diligently worked as a campaign worker for the candidate of his choice. He spoke in President Roosevelt's behalf, campaigning enthusiastically for him. He arranged gala benefits for the Kennedys and was very instrumental in raising huge sums of campaign money which aided greatly in John Fitzgerald Kennedy becoming the 32nd President of the United States. There is a direct quote from Mr. Sinatra on how he viewed himself as an entertainer and how he saw his responsibilities in helping to elect candidates of his choice. "I believe that an entertainer's function is to entertain, but he is also responsible citizen with the same rights and obligations as the next man. I feel it is the duty of every American citizen to help elect the candidates of his choice." [15]

The fifth point of the star is that Mr. Sinatra has always battled against prejudice. When he was growing up in Hoboken, the Italian people dared not to cross beyond Willow Avenue, as they feared deportation. Hoboken was a huge melting pot of Irish, German, Polish and Italian. It was a crowded city of over 70,000 people. My dad, who is still alive, frequently told me about the Willow Terrace where he grew up referring to it as the Demilitarized Zone or DMZ. The terrace was geographically the mid point of Hoboken where everyone regardless of national origin and race finally became assimilated as one people. The Willow Terrace still exists in Hoboken with all nationalities living in harmony.

"When he became a teenage idol, Frank saw a chance to influence young people's views on the racial issue. The only popular singer to speak out on such and explosive subject, Sinatra spoke in high school auditoriums all over the country. He pleaded with students not to dislike others because of their color or religion. Eventually, Sinatra made a short film called "The House I Live In," urging religious and racial tolerance. He donated the proceeds to agencies involved in helping teenagers. In 1946 the film won a special Academy Award." [15] The sixth point of the star is unquestionably that Frank Sinatra is a prophet who has made huge profits from his God given talent. You now have the six points of the star. A singing legend, a gifted actor, a humanitarian and philanthropist, a zealous campaign worker instrumental in electing the candidates of his choice, and the first popular singer to stand against racial and religious prejudice and a prophet who has made huge profits from his God-given talent.

When Jesus returned to his own town of Nazareth, many jealous people came forth in disbelief that this was the same man who was performing such miracles and wondrous things through out the land. The people were offended by him because they couldn't believe a carpenter's son from their own town could be teaching and performing such wondrous acts. They asked him to perform miracles so they can judge if he was truly a prophet. In Chapter 6 from St. Mark in the King James Holy Bible St. Mark states: *"And he could there do no mighty work save that he laid his hands upon a few sick folk and healed them."*

In brief, the people or Nazareth, were not impressed but were offended at him with some resorting to stoning. But Jesus said unto them, *"A prophet is not without honor, but in his own country, and among his own kin, and in his own house."* There will always be jealous people who can not accept those who go out to succeed and make it on their own. In successful people's mind, however, the norm is not to conform. Conformity may insulate you from the

YOUNG FRANK PLAYING POOL AT THE CAT'S MEOW IN HOBOKEN WITH PAT ALTIMORI AND RUNNER FARRISI

(From the Galante collection)

"There'll be times we long for and will miss those days of old"

Mr. Sinatra loved playing pool with his friends in Hoboken at the Cat's Meow.

Below: Frank Sinatra leaving Stevens Institute of Technology in Hoboken after receiving an honorary Doctorate in Engineering on May 23, 1985.

reality's of the world and there is nothing wrong with that. However, one should not criticize others when a person feels he must venture out when they believe in themselves with a burning desire to succeed.

On January 7, 1995, I interviewed Mr. Joe Caporino, who owns Caporino's candy and tobacco store on Adams Street in Hoboken. He told me about his dad, Pop Caporino, who came from Italy at the age of 14 and stayed with the Monaco family, who are related to the Sinatras. Mr. Caporino's dad founded Caporino's over 70 years ago. Joe told me how Dolly and Marty Sinatra use to come in and buy cigarettes and chewing gum. He also told me that Tina Sinatra was recently in his store and saw the gum that Joe still sells that Mr. Sinatra use to enjoy as a boy, which is called Choward's scented gum. Mr. Caporino then asked me if I had ever seen a picture of a young Mr. Sinatra sitting on the banks of the Hudson. As Joe proudly went to get his photo, I knew already what he was going to show me. It was the very picture that inspired my vision over two and half years ago. However, this photo was from the first generation meaning it was the one my Uncle Jimmy Galante had made a photo of over thirty years ago. I thought this was a strange occurrence of fate.

Tina Sinatra was visiting Hoboken because of the new movie she was filming entitled "Hoboken." Also, there was renewed interest that the Frank Sinatra Museum might be coming to Hoboken, New Jersey, since talks with the Smithsonian were now at logger-heads. I recalled the definition of reprise: the return to the first subject or theme of a sonata movement or to repeat or come back.

Finally, Joe Caporino told me I should call Mr. Vince Giusto, who lives in Weehawken, New Jersey. Joe told me that Vince and his wife Marie had many interesting photos of Mr. Sinatra and that I might be able to use them in the book. When I called Vince to tell him of my purpose he asked me to meet him at his house. Astonishingly, he told me that he and his wife had bought the house from Dolly and Mary Sinatra over 30 years ago when the Sinatras decided to move to Fort Lee. When I arrived at 37 King

Avenue on Friday, January 13, 1995, Vince graciously introduced me to his wife Marie (Medici) Giusto. Marie was very interested in my story especially when I told her that Mario, Frank and I met at I'Medici in Atlantic City. The Giusto's proudly showed me post cards they received from Marty and Dolly after they sold their house to them in 1963. Vince then showed me the invitation he received from Dolly and Marty when they renewed their wedding vows after 50 years. He further added that when they bought the house over 30 years ago, "the house was immaculate when they moved in." He then brought me into the dining room and showed me the antique furniture that the Sinatras had sold them, which was well over one hundred years old and an heirloom of the Sinatra family. Vince told me that Mr.Sinatra purchased the home for his parents after his success in the movie "From Here to Eternity." Vince and Marie Giusto would like Mr. Sinatra to know that the house is still maintained in the same immaculate order, the same way it was left to them by his parents.

All great creations begin with imagination. A wise man once said that enthusiasm is the mother of invention and without it nothing great can ever be accomplished. Imagination and enthusiasm are powerful qualities, but one must also have the will and resolution to succeed. One must also have a plan and be focused in to achieve greatness. The final ingredient is hard work or much more perspiration than inspiration. I believe that Frank Sinatra used all of these power qualities in his make up to become the person he is along with being blessed with God given talent. He has been fortunate that he has been gifted to make people happy in a world that needs more happiness now than anytime in our lives. We also need dreamers because without dreams there is no hope.

Therefore, I still dream that Sinatra's "From Here to Eternity" will become a reality in Hoboken. I can still see this splendid hotel with a Sinatra theater for the performing arts along with a Baseball Hall of Fame because baseball was born in this town. In this wonderful hotel I see a bar named "Marty O'Briens " in honor of Frank's Dad and also see a beautiful restaurant named "Dolly's." I see people coming from all over the world to visit our small historic town paying tribute to the greatest star in the world. Where once a young man sat on the banks of the Hudson staring out wondering what life had in store for him, his dreams have been answered by Sinatra's "From Here to Eternity."

Where we still hear those children Christmas morn'
And the flags in parades and blowing horns.

CHAPTER 10

Encore

The Hudson River flows along the town where he was born. He walked the streets in a young boy's dream trying to make it on his own. The day after Christmas a wonderful thing happened! We received a letter on the personalized stationery of Mrs Barbara Sinatra. The letter was dated December 21, which I thought was their way of sending us a most wonderful Christmas gift. On Dec. 20, the Sinatras had returned from a concert tour in Japan so we felt extremely honored that we were remembered. The letter stated that Mr. Sinatra "loved" the song and "loved" everyone involved with his tribute. It went on to say that we had made him "very happy." It was such a warm and touching letter that I felt it was written by Mr. Sinatra, especially when he said, "You did great." It was the greatest present I had ever received— recognition from the Chairman of the Board.

We had brought happiness to a man who has made more people happy through his music than anyone in the world, and at this time, I now feel I have lived for some purpose. We placed a copy of the letter on display at Lepore's for the "city of cold shoulders but a city with a big heart." For the next four days, we played Frank's tribute song constantly while re-reading the letter to make certain it was the real mccoy.

The day after New Years we received a second letter directly from none other than Francis Albert Sinatra. The letter thanked us for the marvelous presentation in chocolate that Mr. Sinatra received at the Sands. However, there was no specific date on the letter other than December 1994 and from Frank's office — not from his home in California. Initially, I thought we were being invited to California to the Seventh Annual Frank Sinatra Celebrity Golf tournament to benefit the Barbara Sinatra's Children's Center in Palm Desert California and thought Mr. Foster and Mr Reardon would be asked to sing his tribute song. When I looked at the post mark on the envelope, I saw that the letter had been run through twice on two different postage meters. It had one date which said Dec. O and another marked December 29. It was very strange since my experience as an executive search consultant left me a little paranoid when it came to letters with double dates.

We proudly displayed both letters at the store along with a copy of the song, "A Time That Was." Since we were still in the holiday season, many people from Hoboken viewed the letters and were very happy that Mr. Sinatra still remembered his hometown. By this time I had written over one hundred pages of "Our Way" and had no intention of stopping my writing especially when I had discovered what an extraordinary individual Dolly Sinatra was in her life time. I wanted to believe that the second letter was from Frank Sinatra but inwardly, I knew what a prolific letter writer Mr. Sinatra was through my research. Also, the second letter sounded nothing like the first one that Barbara and Frank had written to us. Therefore, I was perplexed again.

After I reassessed what had transpired over the last thirty days of trying to get to Sinatra, my conclusion was this: the least likely letter or rocket to reach Sinatra was the one I wrote to Barbara Sinatra at the Childrens Center. The letter arrived at the

Children's Center seven days before Mr. Sinatra's performance at
the Sands on November 17th. This was the letter I sent when the
Mayor was unable to attend Mr. Sinatra's performance. It was also
sent not to upset Mr. Sinatra and possibly destroy the creative
effort, time and money that went into his tribute song.

When the Sinatras attended the annual Christmas party at
the Children's Center on December 13, I believe they received my
letter along with a tape recording of the song and a simple lyric
sheet. In other words Mario's magnificent presentation, which was
last seen by the butler, disappeared or was disassembled for
inspection. If this is the policy of Sinatra Enterprises then I accept
the final outcome since "nobody gets to Sinatra." However, if
someone took it upon their own to discard his genuine tribute
from his city, then these people grossly overstepped their
boundaries. After my conversation with Mr. Frank Sinatra Jr at
I'Medici the night before Mr. Sinatra's performance, I had made
certain to comply with every letter of the law so there would be no
misunderstanding of not going through proper channels.

The beauty and magic of the Sinatra letters is that people
feel Frank has come back to Hoboken. That's enough happiness in
itself, that a letter from Mr. Sinatra can make our city feel alive and
well, remembering that he was born in this town. When I was
boxing chocolates at our store during the Christmas rush, one
gentleman was reading the letter from the Sinatras, as well as the
lyrics to the song. He is a member of what I call the system people
in our city. They have a fat job with the city and do nothing but
criticize any effort that is made by anyone creative and hard
working. Their whole existence is predicated upon collecting a
paycheck and doing the minimal amount of work. These are the
same people that Dolly Sinatra fought when she dared to step
beyond the DMZ zone of Willow Avenue fighting against
injustice. As Shakespeare said: "The players change but the stage
remains the same." After my guest read the letter and the lyrics to
song, he smugly said, "What are you into music now?" The literal
interpretation from his comment was: "You lost running for Mayor

and now you're writing music. Boy are you a loser." I told him proudly that "it took us two and one half years to get to Frank but we finally did!" He then stated in a self assured and conceited fashion: "It took you over two years! We wrote him a letter and in two weeks he sent us a check for $1,000." I must point out that this man was speaking in behalf of a charitable organization, but this guy is a taker. After he spoke so proudly about receiving a check for $1,000, I recalled one of Mr. Sinatra's most fitting songs for the takers: "Here's to the Losers, God Bless them All."

During the last Mayoral campaign in 1993, each candidate was allowed a two minute closing statement. I chose to deliver our 1963 yearbook message that Principal Thomas Gaynor addressed personally to the first graduating class from Hoboken High School. I have tried to live by his beliefs, and I feel Mr. Sinatra would appreciate the values Tom Gaynor tried to instill in all students that entered his school. At this time Mr. Gaynor is still very much alive and these are his words:

"Throughout our lives each of us is called upon to value himself. We place a price tag on our time. We are "worth" so much an hour or a week. We compare ourselves with others to their disadvantage. We feel we are "worth" more on the job than the other fellow; our exploits more worthy of attention and reward.

Each of us has his own measuring stick in deciding personal worth. They are many and varied. But what is a person really worth? Chemically we are worth about five dollars each, but certainly we are worth more than that. Should worth be determined by financial success? Will Rogers once said that "there are many people who think they are worth a lot of money just because they have it." The Rockefellers have been valued not by what they have but by what they have given to others.

The real value of a person consists in giving—not having. Washington, who refused a crown; Lincoln, who died to preserve the nation; the Carpenter's Son of Nazareth; the

Maid of Orleans — their value cannot be measured in currency. Their value is measured by the sacrifices they made for God and country.

You, the Class of January, 1963, are the first to graduate from our magnificent new building — a building which has been valued a more than four million dollars. But this school cannot be valued in terms of money. Its value to the community can only be found by measuring its graduates; measuring them in terms of loyalty and devotion to our nation's ideals; measuring them according to their response to the obligations of a free society; measuring them by their adherence to high ethical and moral standards.

As we wish you good luck and ask God's blessing for your future, we pray that your standards of value will always place honor above wealth, truth above expediency, gentility above vulgar force, and humanity above self.

We hope that these standards will always be yours, and that you will never be found wanting when the question is asked —

What are you worth?

People such as Thomas Gaynor, Dolly, Cookie and Maime never die. Their courage and ideals stay with you. That's if you believe in how they valued worth. I pray Mr. Sinatra will be with us for many more years, because he is a true American hero. He bridges the gap of a time that was and a time that still is! He is the star of stars that came from a small but historic city. Nowhere else but Hoboken, Baseball and Sinatra. That's America to me!

As I step to the podium to pay tribute with "A Time That Was," I close by saying: "Our Way" could never have been written without a song, since I believed so deeply that a song in Mr. Sinatra's honor would make him happy. I will always believe that Frank Sinatra heard his tribute sung by Bruce Stephen Foster on Christmas Eve, especially when his letter said: "You did great!" As they say in show business: ENCORE! ENCORE!

FRANK'S MYSTICAL POSE AT ELYSIAN FIELDS WHERE THE FIRST ORGANIZED GAME OF BASEBALL WAS PLAYED
(From the Galante collection)

"He walked the streets in a young boy's dream trying to make it on his own"

This photo was personally given to Tina Sinatra when she was filming the TV movie, "Sinatra," in 1992.
As fate would have it, the only way I got to Tina was through her camera man who accidentally stumbled into Lepore's looking for a five mile run in Hoboken.

SWIMMING IN THE HUDSON IN HOBOKEN
(from the Galante collection)

"There once was a time that was when life was so simple and wishes came true"

Young Frank Sinatra mystically staring at Nick Gagliardi, who was killed in combat at Lusan in the Phillipines in WWII. Ralph Cotone passed away at 30 years of age is seated up at front of Mr. Sinatra. The two gentlemen above Mr. Sinatra are Dice Verdone, Frank Farisi.

"A Time That Was"

The Hudson River flows along the town where he was born
He walked the streets in a young boy's dream trying to
    make it on his own
Where we still hear those children Christmas morn'
And the flags in parades and blowing horns.
The champagne overflowed New Years Eve in every bar
While our soldiers marched away and boarded ships
    that sail to war
They say a man can never go home—well, we don't believe
    that's true
From Here to Eternity doesn't seem so far, when we feel so
    close to you
Do you remember?
There once was time that was
When life was so simple
Where wishes came true
The road may lead back home again—But till it does
There once was a time that was
There'll be times we long for and will miss those days of old
The families, friends, and memories and the love they
    always hold
You sang every night from your soul
Then God whispered, "Go and tell the world the stories
    you've been told"
So why does a man search for rainbows far away?
Well, this much I've learned is true
When he feels in his heart where life's destiny leads him
He knows what he has to do

And I remember
There once was a time that was
Where life was so simple
Where wishes came true
The road may lead back home again—but till it does
There once was a time that was
And after all of these years, through the triumph and
    the tears
There's still a smile in those ol' eyes of blue
He's the same man but the journey is brand new
Let him tell you his story, let him sing once more for you
And we'll remember
There once was a time that was
When life was so simple
And wishes came true
The road may lead back home again—but till it does
There once was a time that was.

"QUO VADIS, DOMINI?"

STRANGE OCCURRENCES OR ACTS OF FATE

1. Mr. Frank Sinatra and my Uncle Frank Sirocka graduated together from David E. Rue Grammar School in Hoboken and sat right in back of each other. They stand right next to each other in their graduation picture. (see photo).
2. Francis Albert Sinatra was Baptized as Francis at St. Francis Church by mistake.
3. St. Francis of Assisi in New York is where I discovered the book, "Who Moved the Stone" that led me to unearthing the truth about Natalie Sinatra that she was an outstanding woman in Hoboken.
4. Lenny Grandchamp, singer and songwriter in Provincetown, is referred to as the St. Francis of the music business through caring and giving of himself.
5. My Uncle Charlie Romano sang and danced with Dolly Sinatra at 700 Clinton Street in Hoboken, 50 years before Romano's Restaurant was established at the very same site where I interviewed Tony Calabrese when he told me about the Sinatras.
6. The Reprise Logo on Mr. Sinatra's Record Label is almost the exact replica of The City of Hoboken's Gold Seal, both having a steamboat on the seal and logo. Reprise: To return again.
7. A young Frank Sinatra is standing outside of my grandfathers Punch Pflug's plumbing store on 105 Adam Street 70 years ago. (see photo)
8. The Village Inn was the first club Mr. Sinatra sang at in New York I met Jim Reardon and Bruce Foster for the first time at the Village Inn in Point Pleasant over 15 years ago meeting Bruce on Tuesday and Jim on Wednesday.
9. I'm rejected as Mayor at Signore's, the old Continental Lounge. Right across the street, Mr. Sinatra tried many times to sing at the Continental Hotel and met the same fate.
10. Steve Feldman, Tina Sinatra's Cameraman walks into Lepore's by mistake looking for the Onieals Run and saw a picture of

Mr. Sinatra and took me to see Tina because I had negatives to give her and my proposal on Sinatra's "From Here to Eternity."

11. The picture of a young Mr. Sinatra that inspired my vision is traced to one of the original pictures at Mr. Joe Caporino's tobacco and candy store on January 5, 1995.

12. Mr. Caporino tells me of Mr. and Mrs. Vince Giusto, who bought the house on 37 King Street from Dolly and Marty Sinatra. Mr. Giusto's wife's maiden name is Medici, the name of the restaurant Mario, Frank and I met at in Atlantic City. I interview them at 37 King St., previously owned by the Sinatras.

13. The sisters from St. Joe's have come to Lepore's Chocolate since we opened more than 13 years ago. St. Joe's was one of the churches Dolly was very fond of and did a tremendous amount of work for St. Joseph's Home for the Blind.

14. Dolly Sinatra worked as a candy dipper part time for extra money for her family. It is almost identical to the same operation we have at Lepores.

15. The midwives from N.Y., CBS, Carol Barbara and Sally, have been coming to our store every Christmas for 13 years. Dolly Sinatra was a famous mid-wife.

16. I found the picture of Mr. Sinatra resting on top of an old poster of Yankee Stadium signed by Joe DiMaggio to my Uncle Jimmy. Baseball and Sinatra came instantly to my mind.

17. I received a Leroy Nieman print of Mr. Sinatra this Christmas as a gift and in two weeks the same print was used in the Frank Sinatra Society Front cover page. There are thousands of Sinatra photos to choose from. Why this one?

18. When we were at the Sands in Atlantic City on November 17, we met Mr. Singer on the 19th floor when we were trying to deliver our tribute presentation to Mr. Sinatra. Singers Supermarket was the site of the beautiful Fabian Theater located where Mr. Sinatra used to go to the movies when he was a boy in Hoboken as I did. It is now Barnes & Noble Book Store.

19. After the conclusion of Mr. Sinatra's performance at the Sands on November 17, children from St. Ann's in Hoboken, brought flowers to the stage. Ann and Tony Pignotti were present also from Hoboken.

20. The next day Tony Pignotti came to our store. I had never seen him before but recognized him the night before at Mr. Sinatra's Performance, since he sat right next to us. His wife, Ann is a cousin of Manny Action Mateo who chased the Rock Throwers over 50 years ago in Hoboken when they were stoning Mr. Sinatra on stage at St. Ann's in Hoboken.

21. In 1993 I ran for mayor and received 77 votes, and at the time, Mr. Sinatra was 77 years of age. Baltazar Gonzalez, the boy I have legal custody over, wore #77 on April of 1993 when he won the most valuable player in the amateur baseball tournament in Paris, France.

BIBLIOGRAPHY

1. Kennedy, John, "Let the Word Go Forth," New York: Sorensen Theodore, Dela Corte Press 1988, pg 1.

2. John Paul II, "His Holiness, Crossing the Threshold of Hope," Alfred A. Knopf, New York. 1994, pgs. 5, 207 & 211.

3. Roosevelt, Eleanor, "You Learn By Living," Harper and Row, 1960, pgs. 13, 14, 22.

4. City of Hoboken, Hoboken Centenial 1855-1955 Printed by the City of Hoboken, Hoboken Library. 1955, pg. 5.

5. Moller, George, The Hoboken of Yesterday, Hoboken 1964, pgs. 32, 42, 43, 44, 45.

6. Kennedy, John, "Profiles in Courage," New York: Harper Bros., 1956, pg. 246.

7. Juglar, Clement, "Des Commerciales," Paris, 1889, pp. 121.

8. King, John Dr., "How to Profit From the Next Great Depression," N.Y. Penguin, Nal Bank, 1988, pg. 65, 150.

9. Brooks S. Elbridge, "The Central Book of the American Colonies," The Century Company of New York, 1900, pg. 137.

10. Sandberg, Carl, "Chicago," Poems of the Midwest WPC Henry Holt and Co. 1916, Cleveland, Ohio, pg. 27.

11. Kelley, Kitty, "His Way," New York: Bantam Books, 1986, pg. 12, 26, 93 & 95.

12. King James, "The Holy Bible," The Penguin Group, New York: 1974.

13. Morison, Frank, "Who Moved The Stone," Faber & Faber Limited, 1958; Zonderman Publishing House 1958, pg. 18.

14. Ross, Albert Henry, "Who Moved the Stone," 1881. Reprint Faber & Faber, London.

15. Lake, Harriet, "On Stage Frank Sinatra," Creative Education, Mankato, Minn. 1976, pg. 23 & 24.

16. De Palma, Anthony, "Stranger in the Night," New Jersey, Montvill, 1982.*

17. Ringer, Robert, "Million Dollar Habits," Wynwood Press, New York, 1990.*

18. Wilson, Earl "Sinatra," Chicago Macmillan Publishing, 1976.*

* Used as research reading.

INDEX